Improving Teaching and Learning Through Research

Joan S. Stark, *Editor*
University of Michigan

Lisa A. Mets, *Editor*
Northwestern University

NEW DIRECTIONS FOR INSTITUTIONAL RESEARCH

PATRICK T. TERENZINI, *Editor-in-Chief*
University of Georgia

MARVIN W. PETERSON, *Associate Editor*
University of Michigan

Number 57, Spring 1988

Paperback sourcebooks in
The Jossey-Bass Higher Education Series

Jossey-Bass Inc., Publishers
San Francisco • London

Joan S. Stark, Lisa A. Mets (eds.).
Improving Teaching and Learning Through Research.
New Directions for Institutional Research, no. 57.
Volume XV, Number 1.
San Francisco: Jossey-Bass, 1988.

New Directions for Institutional Research is published quarterly by
Jossey-Bass Inc., Publishers (publication number USPS 098-830), and
is sponsored by the Association for Institutional Research. The volume
and issue numbers above are included for the convenience of libraries.
Second-class postage paid at San Francisco, California, and at
additional mailing offices. POSTMASTER: Send address changes to
Jossey-Bass Inc., Publishers, 350 Sansome Street, San Francisco,
California 94104.

Editorial correspondence should be sent to the Editor-in-Chief,
Patrick T. Terenzini, Institute of Higher Education, University of
Georgia, Athens, Georgia 30602.

Library of Congress Catalog Card Number LC 85-645339

International Standard Serial Number ISSN 0271-0579

International Standard Book Number ISBN 1-55542-920-3

Cover art by WILLI BAUM

Manufactured in the United States of America

Ordering Information

The paperback sourcebooks listed below are published quarterly and can be ordered either by subscription or single copy.

Subscriptions cost $48.00 per year for institutions, agencies, and libraries. Individuals can subscribe at the special rate of $36.00 per year *if payment is by personal check.* (Note that the full rate of $48.00 applies if payment is by institutional check, even if the subscription is designated for an individual.) Standing orders are accepted.

Single copies are available at $11.95 when payment accompanies order. (California, New Jersey, New York, and Washington, D.C., residents please include appropriate sales tax.) For billed orders, cost per copy is $11.95 plus postage and handling.

Substantial discounts are offered to organizations and individuals wishing to purchase bulk quantities of Jossey-Bass sourcebooks. Please inquire.

Please note that these prices are for the academic year 1987-88 and are subject to change without notice. Also, some titles may be out of print and therefore not available for sale.

To ensure correct and prompt delivery, all orders must give either the *name of an individual* or an *official purchase order number.* Please submit your order as follows:

Subscriptions: specify series and year subscription is to begin.
Single Copies: specify sourcebook code (such as, IR1) and first two words of title.

Mail orders for United States and Possessions, Latin America, Canada, Japan, Australia, and New Zealand to:
Jossey-Bass Inc., Publishers
350 Sansome Street
San Francisco, California 94104

Mail orders for all other parts of the world to:
Jossey-Bass Limited
28 Banner Street
London EC1Y 8QE

New Directions for Institutional Research Series
Patrick T. Terenzini *Editor-in-Chief*
Marvin W. Peterson, *Associate Editor*

IR1 *Evaluating Institutions for Accountability,* Howard R. Bowen
IR2 *Assessing Faculty Effort,* James I. Doi
IR3 *Toward Affirmative Action,* Lucy W. Sells

IR4 *Organizing Nontraditional Study,* Samuel Baskin
IR5 *Evaluating Statewide Boards,* Robert O. Berdahl
IR6 *Assuring Academic Progress Without Growth,* Allan M. Cartter
IR7 *Responding to Changing Human Resource Needs,* Raul Heist, Jonathan R. Warren
IR8 *Measuring and Increasing Academic Productivity,* Robert A. Wallhaus
IR9 *Assessing Computer-Based System Models,* Thomas R. Mason
IR10 *Examining Departmental Management,* James Smart, James Montgomery
IR11 *Allocating Resources Among Departments,* Paul L. Dressel, Lou Anna Kimsey Simon
IR12 *Benefiting from Interinstitutional Research,* Marvin W. Peterson
IR13 *Applying Analytic Methods to Planning and Management,* David S. P. Hopkins, Roger G. Scroeder
IR14 *Protecting Individual Rights to Privacy in Higher Education,* Alton L. Taylor
IR15 *Appraising Information Needs of Decision Makers,* Carl R. Adams
IR16 *Increasing the Public Accountability of Higher Education,* John K. Folger
IR17 *Analyzing and Constructing Cost,* Meredith A. Gonyea
IR18 *Employing Part-Time Faculty,* David W. Leslie
IR19 *Using Goals in Research and Planning,* Robert Fenske
IR20 *Evaluting Faculty Performance and Vitality,* Wayne C. Kirschling
IR21 *Developing a Total Marketing Plan,* John A. Lucas
IR22 *Examining New Trends in Administrative Computing,* E. Michael Staman
IR23 *Professional Development for Institutional Research,* Robert G. Cope
IR24 *Planning Rational Retrenchment,* Alfred L. Cooke
IR25 *The Impact of Student Financial Aid on Institutions,* Joe B. Henry
IR26 *The Autonomy of Public Colleges,* Paul L. Dressel
IR27 *Academic Program Evaluation,* Eugene C. Craven
IR28 *Academic Planning for the 1980s,* Richard B. Heydinger
IR29 *Institutional Assessment for Self-Improvement,* Richard I. Miller
IR30 *Coping with Faculty Reduction,* Stephen R. Hample
IR31 *Evaluation of Management and Planning Systems,* Nick L. Poulton
IR32 *Increasing the Use of Institutional Research,* Jack Lindquist
IR33 *Effective Planned Change Strategies,* G. Melvin Hipps
IR34 *Qualitative Methods for Institutional Research,* Eileen Kuhns, S. V. Martorana
IR35 *Information Technology: Innovations and Applications,* Bernard Sheehan
IR36 *Studying Student Attrition,* Ernest T. Pascarella
IR37 *Using Research for Strategic Planning,* Norman P. Uhl
IR38 *The Politics and Pragmatics of Institutional Research,* James W. Firnberg, William F. Lasher
IR39 *Applying Methods and Techniques of Futures Research,* James L. Morrison, William L. Renfro, Wayne I. Boucher
IR40 *College Faculty: Versatile Human Resources in a Period of Constraint,* Roger G. Baldwin, Robert T. Blackburn
IR41 *Determining the Effectiveness of Campus Services,* Robert A. Scott
IR42 *Issues in Pricing Undergraduate Education,* Larry H. Litten
IR43 *Responding to New Realities in Funding,* Larry L. Leslie
IR44 *Using Microcomputers for Planning and Management Support,* William L. Tetlow
IR45 *Impact and Challenges of a Changing Federal Role,* Virginia Ann Hodgkinson

IR46 *Institutional Research in Transition,* Marvin W. Peterson, Mary Corcoran
IR47 *Assessing Educational Outcomes,* Peter T. Ewell
IR48 *The Use of Data in Discrimination Issues Cases,* William Rosenthal, Bernard Yancey
IR49 *Applying Decision Support Systems in Higher Education,* John Rohrbaugh, Anne Taylor McCartt
IR50 *Measuring Faculty Research Performance,* John W. Creswell
IR51 *Enhancing the Management of Fund Raising,* John A. Dunn, Jr.
IR52 *Environmental Scanning for Strategic Leadership,* Patrick M. Callan
IR53 *Conducting Interinstitutional Comparisons,* Paul T. Brinkman
IR54 *Designing and Using Market Research,* Robert S. Lay, Jean J. Endo
IR55 *Managing Information in Higher Education,* E. Michael Staman
IR56 *Evaluating Administrative Services and Programs,* Jon F. Wergin, Larry A. Braskamp

The Association for Institutional Research was created in 1966 to benefit, assist, and advance research leading to improved understanding, planning, and operation of institutions of higher education. Publication policy is set by its Publications Board.

For information about the Association for Institutional Research, write:

AIR Executive Office
314 Stone Building
Florida State University
Tallahassee, FL 32306

(904) 644-4470

Contents

Editors' Notes

History may record the 1980s as a decade of emphasis on teaching and learning at all educational levels. In postsecondary education, numerous national reports have focused our attention on educational quality, the processes of teaching and learning, constructing coherent academic programs, documenting evidence of student learning, and fostering the organizational conditions needed to make these issues campus priorities. Maintaining and improving educational quality in colleges and universities requires collaboration among all segments of the academic community.

While a large part of the responsibility for responding to these new challenges rests on the shoulders of faculty and academic administrators, institutional researchers may and should be called upon to play an expanding role in educational improvement. This role includes identifying and defining areas for improvement, suggesting methods of evaluation, collecting data about educational processes, and providing information on which faculty and administrators can base policy decisions. Additionally (this is closely related to their more traditional functions), institutional researchers may be asked to document for external agencies the educational effectiveness of programs and services, as well as their cost-effectiveness.

Since the origin of institutional research in the late 1950s, and because of management demands for budget and enrollment information through the 1960s and 1970s, the study of teaching and learning has not received concentrated attention from institutional researchers. In describing past and current trends in the field at the 25th Anniversary Forum of the Association for Institutional Research (AIR), experienced individuals made it clear that—beyond some descriptive studies of student characteristics, faculty workload, and involvement in academic program review under retrenchment pressures—the study of educational processes has decreased in importance (Fincher, 1985; Peterson, 1985). Three possible reasons for this apparent lack of interest may be the press of noneducational management problems assigned to institutional research offices, reluctance to intrude into territory of the teaching faculty, and the difficult conceptual and measurement problems encountered in studying teaching and learning processes. All of these reasons and others probably have played a part in keeping institutional research studies "quantitative and management-oriented" (Peterson, 1985). These factors will need to be overcome if key college and university administrators are to respond to urgings that the quality of teaching and learning be more fully documented. That they are likely to do so for a host of reasons can be surmised from current activities ranging from Derek Bok's encouragement of an "assessment seminar" for Harvard in 1986 to Northeast Missouri State University's publication of its value-added approach to validate its quality standards.

The new emphasis on teaching and learning processes and outcomes can be viewed as an opportunity. As a new area for research, it provides a vehicle to join institutional researchers and faculty in collaborative activities that serve the institution and its clients. Just as new territory will be explored jointly in generating data useful to faculty and administrative decision makers, institutional researchers will also finally have the chance to demonstrate the utility of existing data that have not been fully exploited. The new role will, however, require institutional researchers to refresh old skills, learn new skills, recreate linkages (discarded in earlier years) with educational researchers (Fincher, 1985, p. 21), and think creatively about their enhanced role and its possibilities. This volume is directed at stimulating creative thinking about new areas for institutional research and at reestablishing contact with some of the ideas being pursued by educational and psychological researchers.

The chapters included in this volume are drawn from the early literature reviews, discussions, and pilot studies of researchers at the National Center for Research to Improve Postsecondary Teaching and Learning (NCRIPTAL) at the University of Michigan (Grant #OERI-G-86-0010). It is more than a coincidence that in 1985 the U.S. Office of Educational Research and Improvement (OERI) funded, for the first time, a research center to study postsecondary teaching and learning, to complement its previous emphasis on developing techniques for institutional management. It is significant, too, that the center's mandate included national leadership, encouraging others suitably situated on college campuses to undertake similar studies. In keeping with that mission, researchers from NCRIPTAL describe in this volume some promising avenues for attention and potential contributions of institutional researchers. Of course, opinions expressed are those of the authors and not of the OERI or the U.S. Government.

From the many conceptual frameworks that might have been chosen to guide their work, NCRIPTAL researchers chose a model in which designated aspects of the collegiate educational environment are viewed as subject to improvement by deliberate and defensible action. As condensed in Figure 1, this guiding framework selects for study five subenvironments in which educational processes are embedded (classroom teaching and learning, curriculum, faculty, institutional context, and technology). Student cognitive and affective characteristics (presaged by their demographic characteristics, goals, and prior learning experiences) are modified when students encounter these aspects of the college envi-

Figure 1. Variables in NCRIPTAL's Research Agenda

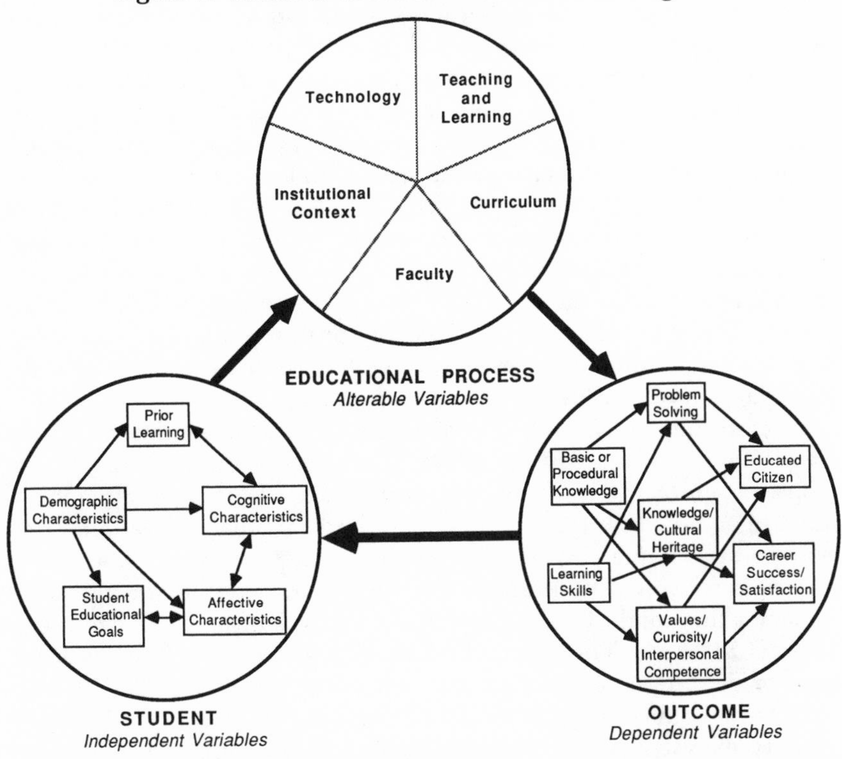

ronment. The results are educational outcomes, ranging from basic skills (short-range outcomes) to career and life accomplishments (long-range outcomes). In general, research conducted at NCRIPTAL seeks to identify variations in educational environments (that is, alterable educational processes) that may be instrumental in modifying the outputs.

Such a focus on altering educational processes may be new to some institutional researchers who have limited their investigations to describing inputs and outputs while ignoring process. An additional departure from familiar models is the idea that an output at one stage of education is an input for the next stage. In Figure 1, this idea is represented by the arrow from the "outcome" circle to the "student" (or "input") circle. In this conception, such characteristics as study skills and learning strategies, motivation for learning, aptitude for learning, and even student educational goals are seen as dynamic rather than static attributes, subject to modification by the educational processes employed. These student outcomes are constantly recycled as education proceeds.

The chapters in this volume offer no panaceas or fully developed new research strategies to institutional researchers. Rather, they highlight how little we know about the processes of teaching and learning in our institutions and the environments in which these processes are embedded. The chapters suggest some critical questions and potential techniques to set the stage for new endeavors.

In the opening chapter, Patricia J. Green and Joan S. Stark examine the broad and diffuse problem of improving college teaching and learning by identifying those junctures at which institutional research seems best prepared to make a contribution and those where considerable groundwork is still needed. Chapter One also serves as an overview of this volume by pointing to new research options that may bear fruit but have been explored heretofore only by "basic" educational researchers. Subsequent chapters move from the macro level of institutional analysis to the micro level of exploring classroom processes and study outcomes. For most institutional researchers, this progression will move from the most familiar to the least familiar territory.

In Chapter Two, Marvin W. Peterson discusses aspects of the academic environment, institutional culture, and institutional climate that appear to influence teaching and learning. At a time when attention is focused on how institutions can improve undergraduate education, Peterson points out the paucity of research that directly connects academic practices with student learning, and he suggests important groups of practices that might be examined in the search for improved learning.

In Chapter Three, Joan S. Stark and Malcolm A. Lowther begin with a definition of *curriculum* as an academic plan or design, constructed at both course and program levels. They narrow in on the potential variables that not only affect faculty's course planning but may also, in turn, affect the types of learning activities experienced by students.

In Chapter Four, Janet H. Lawrence outlines a new direction for research on the faculty teaching role and its meaning. Previous research, some of it conducted by institutional researchers, has implied that improvement should involve either solutions based on incentive systems or those based on correcting "poor" teaching. Lawrence argues for the importance of examining faculty's own perceptions about teaching and their motivations to teach, in order to help institutional leaders and faculty find new and more productive ways to improve teaching and learning.

In Chapter Five, Paul R. Pintrich distills complex findings from cognitive psychology that institutional researchers can use to understand ways of increasing student motivation and cognition, as well as to reveal the relations between these two aspects of learning. Current assessment initiatives may be most successful in improving college learning if they are undergirded by a theoretical framework of the type that Pintrich describes.

Finally, in Chapter Six, Lisa A. Mets and Joan S. Stark highlight important issues facing institutional researchers who are deciding the extent of their involvement in studying and enhancing teaching and learning. The authors' view is that the case for research on teaching and learning is compelling, and that such research provides opportunities for continued maturation of the institutional research profession. The authors also describe some self-study tools, currently being developed at NCRIPTAL, that are potentially useful to campus leaders and institutional researchers. Some recent bibliographical sources also are described.

In the preface to the *New Directions for Institutional Research* volume coinciding with the twenty-fifth anniversary of the Association for Institutional Research, Peterson and Corcoran state: "Our view is that institutional research has succeeded in large measure because it has historically been on the cutting edge of new and emerging challenges to institutions of higher education and because it has helped them to adapt to those challenges" (1985, p. 1). We hope that this volume will illuminate provocative issues that will help institutional researchers remain on the "cutting edge" in an area of research that is at the heart of higher education.

Joan S. Stark
Lisa A. Mets
Editors

References

Fincher, C. "The Art and Science of Institutional Research." In M. W. Peterson and M. Corcoran (eds.), *Institutional Research in Transition.* New Directions for Institutional Research, no. 46. San Francisco: Jossey-Bass, 1985.

Peterson, M. W. "Institutional Research: An Evolutionary Perspective." In M. W. Peterson and M. Corcoran (eds.), *Institutional Research in Transition.* New Directions for Institutional Research, no. 46. San Francisco: Jossey-Bass, 1985.

Peterson, M. W., and Corcoran, M. "Editors' Notes." In M. W. Peterson and M. Corcoran (eds.), *Institutional Research In Transition.* New Directions for Institutional Research, no. 46. San Francisco: Jossey-Bass, 1985.

Joan S. Stark is professor of higher education, researcher in the Center for the Study of Higher and Postsecondary Education, and director of the National Center for Research to Improve Postsecondary Teaching and Learning (NCRIPTAL), at the University of Michigan.

Lisa A. Mets is assistant to the vice-president for administration and planning at Northwestern University. She is currently a doctoral candidate in higher education at the University of Michigan and was formerly a research associate in the Center for the Study of Higher and Postsecondary Education and the National Center for Research to Improve Postsecondary Teaching and Learning (NCRIPTAL), at the University of Michigan.

In addition to pursuing studies for which they are best qualified, institutional researchers could play a key role in linking basic, policy, and evaluation research to improve teaching and learning.

Collaborative Roles in Improving Postsecondary Teaching and Learning

Patricia J. Green, Joan S. Stark

During the 1980s, discussion about education has shifted from issues of access and equality toward a concern with realizing the potential for achievement among students at all levels of preparation and ability. There is widespread discussion about the meaning of excellence in postsecondary education and the varied routes of its achievement. In such a climate, both new research and new policies can assist in improving credibility and accountability in collegiate education. These trends suggest a unique opportunity for institutional research to extend cooperative campus relationships and to inform and contribute to policy development.

Since the approaches employed by both researchers and policy-makers are determined by the issues addressed and the specific questions asked, it is essential to assess carefully the types of institutional research that may be most useful in this new era. While making no claim to have identified all possible issues or approaches, in this chapter we explore briefly some of the underlying questions involved in research intended to improve teaching and learning. We consider these questions with respect to the types of research focused on them most frequently in the past. Finally, we consider the potential of institutional research for meeting

J. S. Stark and L. A. Mets (eds.). *Improving Teaching and Learning Through Research.*
New Directions for Institutional Research, no. 57. San Francisco: Jossey-Bass, Spring 1988.

expanded demands for new information, and we conclude that improvement will require collaboration among very different types of researchers who may inform and enhance one another's efforts. While institutional researchers are not in a position to undertake all the needed research directly, they can play a key role in linking these diverse efforts with policy development at the campus and state levels.

Potential Intervention Points to Improve Teaching and Learning

When research is intended to guide changes that will improve student learning, different strategies for improvement suggest themselves at each of several levels. In this chapter we will consider four levels at which research-based interventions might produce improvements in student outcomes.

One approach to the complex problem of improvement is to view the *activities* of teaching and learning either as distinct or as mutually dependent activities amenable to research and improvement. To define and clarify productive learning processes and to describe more fully what constitutes effective teaching strategies are important research tasks. A second approach is to focus on the *actors,* rather than upon activities, and examine specific characteristics of teachers and learners that might be key to needed improvements. Among both students and faculty, for example, motivation, involvement, ability, and preparation surely have an impact on the way in which teaching and learning occur. An alternative formulation is to examine the strengths and weaknesses of *formal organizations* for providing teaching and learning, including their effects on activities and actors. Finally, it may be important to obtain greater consensus among administrators, faculty, students, and employers about what is important to learn. Lack of consensus about educational purpose has been exacerbated by long-standing neglect of ways to measure learning and must be addressed if we are to document improved outcomes resulting from curricular change. In our discussion, we will touch briefly on each of these potential intervention points in improving teaching and learning; other authors in this volume will explore them in detail.

Types of Research

Currently, there are at least four interrelated types of research into issues in higher education. Although these types of research overlap and sometimes are confused in public discussions, each has distinctive aspects, and each is likely to play an important role in informing improvement efforts.

First, *basic research* typically is carried out by scholar-researchers in such disciplines as psychology, education, and other social sciences. Its primary purpose is to discover causal relationships concerning the processes of teaching and learning and the various influences on them. Results usually appear in scholarly journals, often without clearly stated implications for change.

Institutional research usually refers to studies carried out by colleges attempting to understand and improve their own activities. Most such studies are descriptive or correlational, and, since they are designed for local use, they are not widely circulated. Only recently have the institutional priorities that direct the work of the institutional research (IR) office focused on the educational process.

Policy analysis is a process of locating and weighing relevant information in order to select strategies likely to produce optimum (or at least acceptable) results. In education, policy analysis examines alternative policies and practices at many levels. For example, faculty committees or department administrators may weigh the merits of strategies directly related to student learning, while institutional researchers are concerned with campuswide policies supporting the educational program. External groups, such as state coordinating agencies and legislatures, choose among alternative strategies and policies that affect entire educational systems. What is most desirable is that all of these analyses draw on results from both basic and institutional research and explicitly use such research to assert that, on the basis of the evidence, selected strategies should be adopted. Although reports of policy research often carry the weight of authority and are circulated widely, the research on which they draw and the basis on which alternatives are chosen are not always made clear.

Evaluative research can be used to study the effects of implementing strategies derived from the other types of research—basic research, institutional research, or policy analysis—by identifying the intended or unintended outcomes that can be attributed to these policies and strategies. Evaluative research may be undertaken by trained professionals or by interested groups and committees with no special research training. Examples include accreditation and both formal and informal program reviews. Since the values and interests of various stakeholders who sponsor the evaluation are important, even evaluation experts often use eclectic methods. Similarly, the extent to which research reports and methodologies are available depends upon both the scope of responsibility and the public accountability of the sponsor. The relation of institutional research to evaluation also varies, ranging from full IR responsibility for conducting an evaluation to providing clerical or data-analysis support for outside evaluators.

A successful program of research for improving teaching and learning will arguably consider the potential contributions of all four types of research. Ideally, the policy analysts would weigh their initial recommendations against knowledge produced by both basic and institutional researchers, while the evaluative researcher would help to supply new and refined questions for both groups of researchers and for policy analysts.

To aid in considering the current status of research on postsecondary teaching and learning, we have created a matrix (see Figure 1) based on the four types of research just described and the several potential intervention points for improving teaching that we mentioned earlier. In the discussion that follows, we assess research activities, trends, and roles in each cell of the matrix and indicate the current and potential involvement of institutional researchers.

The Activities: Learning and Teaching

Learning. If we are to improve learning, we need to consider what it is and how it takes place. All learning involves changes in the learners' ways of thinking and behaving. Interest in the commonalities among different types of learning has now been revitalized by advances in cognitive psychology.

Current basic research on learning attempts to define and conceptualize across types of learning the processes by which individuals amass information and compare, sort, structure, evaluate, and apply it in appropriate or novel ways. Some key factors in an information-processing model of student learning, such as problem-solving abilities, knowledge representation, motivation, and student anxiety, are being more fully identified and measured (see Chapter Five). As the relationships among

Figure 1. Locus of Research to Improve Teaching and Learning

INTERVENTION POINT	BASIC RESEARCH	INSTITUTIONAL RESEARCH	POLICY ANALYSIS	EVALUATION RESEARCH
Activity: Learning Teaching				
Actors: Learners Teachers				
Organization				
Learning Content				

these factors are identified, the possibility of manipulating and altering them through instruction opens the possibility that students can learn to learn. A far different application is to use knowledge about the ways in which people think and learn to structure and sequence material for learning.

Other strands of research on learning within cognitive psychology build on the idea that intellectual development proceeds in stages (Case, 1985; Perry, 1970). In such a research tradition, the key questions involve identifying and facilitating movement from one stage of intellectual development to another. At a more basic level, researchers are examining the relationship between affect and cognition (Zajonc, 1980). Extending these theories to educational research would lead us to explore affective components of the learning situation in order to understand how information learned might be triggered and used in future settings. Last, we might mention that scientific attempts to distinguish and categorize patterns of brain activity might ultimately enable us to relate these patterns to modes of thinking. Such an approach is obviously quite different from traditional categorizations of learning based on societal purposes. All of these current explorations have broad implications for involving students in their learning experiences, as well as for developing continued motivation to undertake new learning.

Clearly, research models such as these, which seek to understand the nature of learning, lie within the realm of basic research, typically in psychology or neuroscience. The exploration of these ideas is painstakingly specialized, and the time needed for translation into practice is lengthy. Unfortunately, since policymakers find it difficult to assess new findings, an incompletely developed theory occasionally emerges into public view and is adopted as a panacea, usually followed by considerable disappointment. Since the long-range potential for these directions in basic research is great, institutional researchers have a role in lobbying against hasty adoption or misdirected adaptations.

Teaching. While learning may be studied as a process in its own right, the process of teaching is difficult to study without specifying a learner. Nevertheless, at least four interrelated dimensions of the teaching task are amenable to study: (1) motivating students to learn, (2) selecting and organizing facts, concepts, principles, skills, and attitudes to be introduced, (3) transmitting knowledge, and (4) serving as a formal or informal role model for students. Recently, an important fifth dimension has been proposed by Cross (1986), who has suggested that all teachers should conduct research directed at improving their own teaching behavior.

In contrast to research on learning, the majority of research on postsecondary teaching has been of an applied, rather than basic, nature, and it frequently has used student evaluations as a primary source of data. Most studies have attempted to evaluate the effectiveness of various methods of transmitting information (see, for example, Braskamp, Brandenburg, and Ory, 1984). This line of research has produced equivocal results; it appears that the most effective mode of teaching depends strongly on the nature of the desired learning outcomes and the type of learner. Although evaluations of teaching by college students indicate that attention to other dimensions is highly valued by them, there is considerably more speculation and less actual research on the remaining dimensions of motivation, selection and organization of instructional content, and role modeling. If psychological or sociological underpinnings of the teaching role exist, as they surely must, they have not yet been identified, nor have they become the province of any discipline for basic research.

The Institutional Research Role. Since much of the work on understanding learning and teaching as activities is likely to be of a basic nature, only those institutional research offices that can employ specialized research personnel are likely to be directing these studies. Nevertheless, we suggest some important roles for institutional researchers. The institutional research staff might profitably develop relationships with the cognitive psychologists on campus, who will alert them to emerging lines of research and fruitful new results. Such individuals can serve as "spotters" for new ideas that might be field-tested, while the IR office reciprocates by serving as a broker and facilitator for basic researchers who need field-test sites. The potential of the new psychological research is sufficiently great that institutional researchers should help to interpret its possibilities to policymakers.

An equally important task for the institutional researcher is to be vigilant about local or state policy decisions that seem to incorporate ideas from basic research either prematurely or so extensively that appropriate evaluation is precluded. Careful selection of target groups for new approaches and the maintenance of control procedures in educational experimentation can build an effective alliance between institutional and basic researchers that advances educational research in general.

Institutional researchers can play an expanding role in teaching. In the past, institutional researchers primarily have developed descriptions of instructional patterns at their institutions. These include number, types, and sizes of classes, modes of instruction, utilization of various campus facilities, grading options, selection of certain courses by students with given majors, and data banks for student evaluations that can be correlated with teacher characteristics. In postsecondary education the teaching process itself, however, has seldom been explored, and there seems a clear need for basic research. Perhaps because of the lack of data, policy analysts (including faculty committees, faculty union leaders, and legislators) have felt quite free to formulate recommendations for improving teaching on the basis of limited applied research in this area. Once policy decisions have been formulated, evaluation often takes on the characteristics of negotiation, rather than research.

As we begin to know more about teaching than ever before, cross-campus collaboration becomes even more essential. Institutional researchers and faculty members might work together to develop mutual respect and a base of knowledge about the process of teaching so that they can jointly assist policy analysts in making informed decisions.

The Actors: Learners and Teachers

Learners. The bulk of our current understanding of teaching and learning stems from extensive research on individual student characteristics. This research might be classified as following two distinct approaches. The first approach, often using large-scale survey data, attempts to describe successful learners and identify the correlates of their success. The second approach is concerned with understanding student learning in relation to student identity, placing the learning experience in the context of students' past abilities and perceived futures.

The first approach asks, "What is it about some students that allows them to succeed at educational tasks?" This question implies that if we understand the characteristics that foster success, we can promote the development of those characteristics that are within our capacity to alter. During recent history, such investigations have been guided by varied theoretical perspectives on student development. Currently popular approaches to the study of student characteristics and learning outcomes attend to the concept of involvement (Astin, 1985), to development of problem-solving abilities, and to the level of student effort (Pace, 1984). The techniques used in such survey studies are well known and useful to institutional researchers. Such studies can take into account unique institutional missions, characteristics, and student clienteles. Nevertheless, their use demands careful interpretation, since the statistical procedures or large sample sizes typically employed can produce results that are trivial or have little utility.

A quite different perspective on individual learners proceeds from another question: "What is the meaning of learning for the learners?" This type of research, focusing on the study of learning as an event in an individual's life history, is exemplified by intensive exploration and synthesis of student perspectives (Chickering, 1969; Perry, 1970; Katchadourian and Boli, 1985). The intensive study of individual learning experiences is also linked to studies in cognitive psychology, where basic researchers have been engaged in studies to define and measure individual "schemata," or cognitive generalizations, about the self for various social roles (Markus, 1977). Application of this type of research might aid in understanding what happens when students incorporate a sense of their ability to learn into their larger identity.

Teachers. For most questions one may ask about learners, parallel questions may be asked about teachers. What differentiates successful from less successful teachers? What is the meaning of teaching for teachers? What promotes their involvement, quality of effort, or productivity?

Demographic descriptions of the college faculty abound and contain information regarding their backgrounds, career events, and political attitudes. Many institutional files also contain extensive correlational data regarding how instructional efforts are viewed by students, but efforts to determine which faculty are successful teachers have been limited by lack of consensus on the criteria to be used. Thus, none of these data banks informs us about which attributes and skills of teachers are important in determining student performance. Further, since policy development regarding faculty roles frequently becomes politicized, the substantial research on the psychology of work in other fields has not been systematically extended to the unique role of the college teacher. Basic researchers collect attitudinal data from faculty about political and social issues or track their careers in terms of institutional prestige, while institutional research offices have collected work-related demographics.

The Institutional Research Role. At least in large institutions, increasingly sophisticated survey research of an ex post facto nature concerning both faculty and students is frequently conducted by IR offices. Although longitudinal studies primarily have been conducted by basic researchers or large-scale research organizations, colleges now are beginning to conduct their own longitudinal studies. Policy analysis drawing on such findings has just begun to emerge, exemplified by the recent report *Involvement in Learning* (NIE Study Group, 1984), which drew upon both national and local studies. If past trends and experience indicate future directions, institutional researchers probably will continue to be more directly involved in studies of learners than in studies of teachers, yet growing interest in studies of faculty may parallel an earlier time in the 1950s, when student studies were in their infancy. Certainly, some recent institutional and state-level proposals for faculty development are based on studies such as that conducted by Bowen and Schuster (1986).

The study of student and faculty characteristics and the derivation of policy implications have developed to the stage where evaluation research is needed to confirm or revise these notions in light of intervention strategies they suggest. We suggest that institutional researchers enter a new era of evaluation research, pursuing the results of interventions based on previous studies of learning characteristics. Thus, IR offices would be in a position to counter global conclusions drawn from nonrigorous studies.

In contrast, studies that explore the meaning of education to students are usually driven by desire for deeper understanding of human experience. Since institutional researchers have neither the time nor the resources to pursue these intensive types of research, the initiative probably should remain with basic researchers. Institutional researchers may play an important role, however, in stimulating the interest of appropriate faculty members and counselors to collect and interpret these kinds of data. The IR office can frequently identify questions that foster more complete understanding and generalization of results to subgroups of students. Furthermore, the IR office may wish to keep informed of all ethnographic or phenomenological studies being conducted of students on the campus. Results of such studies, when corroborated by other data, often have the human appeal needed to bring about change.

Currently, policy researchers at colleges, like researchers in broader settings, have little meaningful information concerning the faculty as teachers. In the absence of such information, and because of the politicization of criterion research by stakeholders, evaluation research languishes. It deserves revitalization. Negotiation of responsibility for this task may well be an important goal for institutional researchers in the years immediately ahead.

Organization of Postsecondary Teaching and Learning

If we seek ways to improve learning, it is reasonable that we scrutinize the institutions that foster student learning as a primary goal. How do these institutions promote or hinder student success?

For many years, both basic and institutional researchers have been engaged in organizational analyses. These studies include early comparisons of statistics among institutions, functional analyses of educational systems (Parsons, Platt, and Smelser, 1973), and recent extensive taxonomies of college goals (Bowen, 1977; Lenning, Lee, Micek, and Service, 1977). They have also included studies of resource allocation systems, sources, and resolutions of political conflict (Zusman, 1986), and models of salary equity among employees. While basic researchers have attempted to understand the characteristics of colleges as organizations, institutional researchers have collected data primarily to facilitate interinstitutional comparisons.

An approach to studying the question of organizational effectiveness might include development of criteria for judging whether postsecondary institutions achieve their multiple goals. Yet, despite diverse approaches to characterizing organizational effectiveness, there has been little attempt in higher education to link the various dimensions of this concept directly to teaching and learning (see Chapter Two). Rather, the dependent variables in studies that purport to measure effectiveness are typically no more complex than satisfaction and morale of alumni or staff.

In the absence of concrete studies, permissible speculation ranges from the thought that organization has no effect on teaching and learning to the assertion that it is necessary to define and measure new aspects of organizational character, such as academic climate. The absence of institutional-level findings thus far has led some researchers to suggest that the new research efforts should be targeted at the suborganizational levels, such as departments or programs (Pascarella, 1985). Others suggest the wholesale construction of new measures of teaching and learning that have greater potential for discriminating among institutions with varying organizational characteristics.

The Institutional Research Role. Currently, considerable impetus for research is being generated by policy analysts in response to public views that strong links exist between organizational effectiveness and teaching and learning. For the institutional researcher, this view suggests a substantial need to replicate research at the institutional or subinstitutional level. Despite the intuitive appeal of organizational change as the vehicle for improving teaching and learning, and despite the strong push of state and national calls for institutional assessment, the development of research models to adequately test this potential relationship lies in the future.

Curriculum Content: Defining What Is to Be Learned

A focus on what is to be learned in college returns this analysis to a point closely related to our initial discussion of learning as a process. Some policy researchers have proposed that learning might be improved if research articulated more clearly what students should learn in colleges and universities and then measured that learning. As this strategy is contemplated, at least five questions must be addressed: What should students learn? Who should decide? Should all students learn the same things? How should we measure what has been learned? What is measurement likely to tell us about which interventions will improve learning?

The first three of these are normative questions. Although lists of desirable learning outcomes are seldom short, they can be broadly classified into three categories: conceptual and factual knowledge, critical thinking and problem-solving skills, and professional or career skills. Setting aside both societal and institutional difficulties in resolving the priorities among these outcomes, institutional researchers can join with evaluative researchers (for example, testing agencies, program review committees, and accreditors) in helping to assess which courses and programs foster each of these sets of objectives. Viewed in this way, the three normative questions are closely linked to the fourth and fifth questions, which institutional researchers, experienced in measurement, can readily help to answer. The answers may and should affect the answers to the first three questions.

To illustrate, if facts and concepts are important, curriculum research should be aimed at designing courses and programs so as to make the information presented easy for students to grasp and assimilate. If critical thinking is the major objective, courses and researchers should investigate how topics can be chosen and organized to purposefully develop these skills. If marketable skills are important, choices of what should be taught may hinge on continual analysis of changing employment needs.

Perennial discussion about what should be learned, coupled with professorial autonomy in the classroom, has tended to suppress controlled curricular experimentation that might help answer normative questions on bases other than personal experiences of decision makers. Meanwhile, decisions about what is to be learned are influenced and made daily by federal and state funders or regulators, employers, accreditors, college programs, families, individual students, faculty members, and administrators. This is an area where institutional researchers can stake out new territory to meet their institutions' demands for new data.

The Institutional Research Role. Institutional researchers might work more intensively with program planners for increased attention to the specific effects of certain types of curricular experiences. Outcome variables might include student involvement, effort, and motivation, as well as facts, principles, skills, and attitudes. Emerging basic and institutional research focusing on student course-taking patterns should tell us what courses students are selecting or avoiding and why. The study of particular subcultures, especially vocationally oriented subcultures, should help us to understand the motivations for student involvement. Such research will require considerably more evaluation on the part of IR offices, as well as more collaboration with faculty program planners than heretofore has been the case.

Observations

Proceeding from our sense of the status quo, we have observed the following.

1. Basic research on college student learning is advancing rapidly through progress in neuroscience and cognitive psychology. At present, these findings frequently are not field-tested or translated into practice. Institutional researchers might well develop specific contacts in these research areas who will keep them abreast of new developments and who can think creatively about the practical implications of these research areas for college learning.

2. The field of research on college teaching is underdeveloped. While attempted improvements in practice proceed by trial and error in scattered settings, little basic knowledge about the teaching process is

available to inform us about the potential impact of intervention through changes in the way teachers teach. As external groups increasingly tend to make erroneous assumptions about college teachers, faculty members and institutional researchers may be more highly motivated to collaborate in answering some of the most basic questions.

3. An abundant literature on student characteristics describes the ways in which students change during college and the correlates of student success. This descriptive and correlational research has reached a stage of development where colleges can readily collect and analyze their own data for policy analysis or for program evaluation. One new task of institutional research is to demonstrate the utility of such data collection to policymaking within the college.

4. Only recently has basic research been launched to explore the meaning of education to the student. Such studies, closely allied to developing psychological paradigms and ethnographic research methods, are expensive and rare. Institutional researchers should become familiar with the techniques and the appeal of such studies in order to encourage selected faculty members and counselors in their collaborative pursuit.

5. Demographic and attitudinal descriptions of faculty members abound. Compared to the parallel database on students, this area of research on faculty lacks longitudinal and correlational studies concerning variables directly linked to the person as teacher. Without realizing the superficiality of research on faculty, policy researchers call on it for propositions that modify the context in which faculty members perform the teaching role. Institutional researchers need to help phrase questions that are meaningful in understanding the role of the teacher.

6. Within the substantial amount of literature on organizations, colleges and universities have received their share of attention from both basic and institutional researchers. Despite this research base, the connections between student learning and varied measures of organizational effectiveness have not been adequately explored. New models are needed for research at all levels, particularly since some researchers advocate seeking meaning through the examination of institutional subcultures, while assessment policy initiatives increasingly move to a broader systemwide or statewide context.

7. Partly because consensus is lacking about what students should learn, partly because of beliefs in individual choice, and partly because research has been politicized, there are few models to identify the differences between what students are supposed to learn and what they do learn under varied circumstances. In this arena, keen interest among policy and evaluation researchers may stimulate more basic investigations in which institutional researchers can play an aggressive role.

Conclusions

As a heuristic device, we have separated several ways of approaching the task of improving teaching and learning and considered them in light of four types of research that might provide enlightenment. It quickly becomes obvious that each juncture at which teaching and learning might be improved is inextricably related to the others. One of the benefits of examining each as a discrete issue is that we are then able to see the relationships and the needs for collaboration in research more clearly.

While the relationships between teacher and learner, teaching and learning, goals and outcomes are commonly recognized, the connections between the types of research we have described are not so obvious. If, as some assert, educational research has little impact on practice, the reason may be that links among the various types of research, often undertaken by diverse agencies for varying purposes, are weak or nonexistent. Therefore, we set forth some recommendations about how this situation could be brought closer to the ideal.

The potentially desirable relationship among various types of research is diagrammed in Figure 2. This system currently does not operate ideally for many segments of higher education. The responsibility for developing a more integrated strategy for using the various types of research on campuses should be accepted by institutional researchers. Here we offer some suggestions for future directions in each area.

1. Basic research that holds promise of improving college teaching and learning needs greater support, broader field-testing, and improved translation for the use of institutional researchers. It is no secret that much of this research originated as psychologists explored various aspects of personality and cognition with the most convenient subjects, college students. Colleges themselves have never invested heavily in the research-

Figure 2. Ideal Relationship Among Existing Types of Research

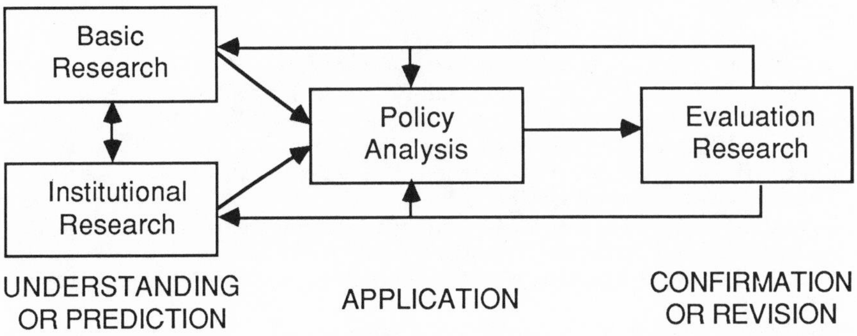

and-development enterprise geared toward improving teaching. Societal interest, as well as institutional self-interest, make this a propitious time to foster greater amounts of such research.

2. Institutional research typically has focused on aspects of organization most closely allied to funding, facilities and enrollment planning, systems operations, and report generation. In relatively few universities are institutional research personnel either appropriately trained or inclined to apply basic research to the improvement of teaching and learning. In some universities, a separate office of faculty instructional development also exists. In order for the research mechanism to run smoothly, it is time for these offices to join forces and carry out the translation and field-testing function. This type of joint effort could also facilitate the training of faculty members to be classroom researchers, as suggested by Cross (1986).

3. Policy researchers need to weigh basic studies and related field-tests more heavily, recognizing that simplistic alternatives based on superficial understanding are unlikely to provide long-range improvements. Even so, if the necessary developmental mechanisms for basic research and institutional field-testing do not exist, policy researchers can hardly be blamed for choosing among what seem promising available studies.

4. Last, despite objections on grounds of intrusion, institutions need to sponsor carefully structured evaluation research. Traditionally, universities have relied primarily on policy analysis, such as sporadic efforts of faculty committees to collect descriptive data about teaching and learning and to develop recommended changes. The institutional research office in a university should have a threefold obligation: to assist in gathering information for policy analysis, to evaluate the results of chosen policy alternatives, and to identify areas of need for new basic and institutional research. Such an office would complete the link in a systematic research enterprise that would at least approach the complexity of the problems by which it is challenged.

References

Astin, A. W. *Achieving Educational Excellence: A Critical Assessment of Priorities and Practices in Higher Education.* San Francisco: Jossey-Bass, 1985.

Bowen, H. R. *Investment in Learning: The Individual and Social Value of American Higher Education.* San Francisco: Jossey-Bass, 1977.

Bowen, H. R., and Schuster, J. *American Professors: A National Resource Imperiled.* New York: Oxford University Press, 1986.

Braskamp, L., Brandenburg, D. C., and Ory, J. C. *Evaluating Teaching Effectiveness: A Practical Guide.* Newbury Park, Calif.: Sage, 1984.

Case, R. *Intellectual Development: Birth to Adulthood.* Orlando, Fla.: Academic Press, 1985.

Chickering, A. W. *Education and Identity.* San Francisco: Jossey-Bass, 1969.

Cross, K. P. *The Need for Classroom Research.* Ann Arbor: National Center for Research to Improve Postsecondary Teaching and Learning, The University of Michigan, 1986.

Katchadourian, H. A., and Boli, J. *Careerism and Intellectualism Among College Students: Patterns of Academic and Career Choice in the Undergraduate Years.* San Francisco: Jossey-Bass, 1985.

Lenning, O. T., Lee, Y. S., Micek, S. S., and Service, A. L. *A Structure for the Outcomes of Postsecondary Education.* Boulder, Colo.: National Center for Higher Education Management Systems, 1977.

Markus, H. "Self-Schemata and Processing Information about the Self." *Journal of Personality and Social Psychology,* 1977, *35,* 151–175.

NIE Study Group on the Conditions of Excellence in American Higher Education. *Involvement in Learning: Realizing the Potential of American Higher Education.* Washington, D.C.: U.S. Government Printing Office, 1984.

Pace, C. R. *Measuring the Quality of College Student Experiences: An Account of the Development and Use of the College Student Experiences Questionnaire.* Los Angeles: Higher Education Research Institute, University of California–Los Angeles, 1984.

Parsons, T., Platt, G. M., and Smelser, N. J. *The American University.* Cambridge, Mass.: Harvard University Press, 1973.

Pascarella, E. T. "College Environmental Influences on Learning and Cognitive Development: A Critical Review and Synthesis." In J. Smart (ed.), *Higher Education: Handbook of Theory and Research.* Vol. 1. New York: Agathon, 1985.

Perry, W. G. *Forms of Intellectual and Ethical Development in the College Years: A Scheme.* New York: Holt, Rinehart & Winston, 1970.

Zajonc, R. "Feeling and Thinking: Preferences Need No Inferences." *American Psychologist,* 1980, *35,* 151–175.

Zusman, A. "Legislature and University Conflict: The Case of California." *Review of Higher Education,* 1986, *9,* 397–418.

Patricia J. Green is assistant director of the National Center for Research to Improve Postsecondary Teaching and Learning (NCRIPTAL), at the University of Michigan.

Joan S. Stark is professor of higher education, researcher in the Center for the Study of Higher and Postsecondary Education, and director of the National Center for Research to Improve Postsecondary Teaching and Learning (NCRIPTAL), at the University of Michigan.

Institutional research that examines the influence of organizational and administrative factors on student learning may be critical in improving educational performance.

The Organizational Environment for Student Learning

Marvin W. Peterson

As organizations deliberately created to foster student learning, colleges and universities can identify three important gaps in their research about themselves. First, there is almost no research in which aspects of the organizational and administrative environments of an institution are viewed as predictor variables, and in which improved teaching or improved student academic learning outcomes are seen as the primary dependent variables. Substantial research suggests that the extent of higher education and the types of institution attended (including various institutional characteristics such as size, wealth, and selectivity) affect student attitudes and behaviors (Bowen, 1977; Pascarella, 1985), but little research has examined the internal organizational and administrative dynamics that may lead to such effects. Strong, intensive, and positive institutional climates (such as those often found in small distinctive colleges) can influence student behavior and attitudes; faculty attitudes, roles, and productivity; the external image of the institution; and many other important dependent variables. However, almost none of the climate research reports an impact of climate on student learning (Peterson and others, 1986). Finally, scholarly research on departmental organization and administra-

J. S. Stark and L. A. Mets (eds.). *Improving Teaching and Learning Through Research.*
New Directions for Institutional Research, no. 57. San Francisco: Jossey-Bass, Spring 1988.

tion (Smart and Montgomery, 1976) seldom focuses on student learning as an outcome variable.

A second gap, paralleling that in scholarly research, also exists, in part because institutional research studies for single institutions do not examine the differential impacts of environment.

A third gap in research is a result of confusion in the concepts and terms used to describe organizational variables and characteristics. Terms like *environment, culture,* or *climate,* and the many other organizational variables that regularly are used to describe organizational dynamics, are seldom defined consistently and are often measured quite differently in varied college settings.

Despite these three research gaps, common sense tells us that colleges and universities, as organizations purposefully designed to promote teaching and learning, vary in many important ways. Faculty and administrators do deliberately attempt to create organizational and administrative approaches (beyond classroom settings) to improve teaching and student learning, and some of these attempts do make a difference.

Using these three research gaps as a stimulus, this chapter first presents a framework that researchers might use to help conceptualize organizational and administrative factors that affect student learning in their institutions (Peterson, Cameron, Alexander, and others, 1987). Second, it suggests some important issues that institutional researchers should address in thinking about the organizational and administrative environment for enhancing student learning. Third, it comments on the role that institutional researchers might play in reducing semantic confusion and enhancing understanding of how colleges and universities improve student learning.

The Organizational and Administrative Context: A Framework for Research

It is helpful to conceive of colleges and universities as consisting of seven different overlapping environments: the student, faculty, curricular, educational technological, organizational, administrative, and external environments. (The term *environment* is used here broadly to refer to all organizational phenomena within a prescribed boundary; see Figure 1.) Student, faculty, and administrative environments include the three major groups of actors and their characteristics and behavior. The curricular and educational technology environments refer, respectively, to knowledge structures and delivery modes of teaching and learning. The external environment includes influential individuals, groups, or organizations outside colleges and universities. In this context, organizational environments are viewed as those organized activities (policies, procedures, and practices) that link the other six environments. However, since

Figure 1. College and University Environments

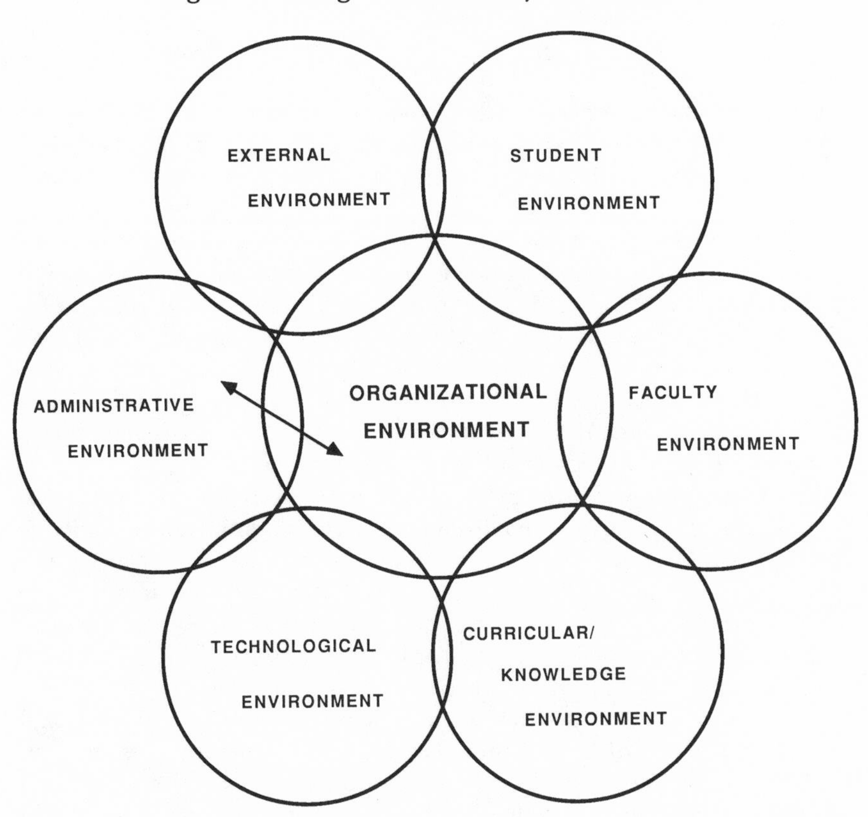

organizational activities and administrative patterns overlap substantially, these two environments are considered as one. This chapter focuses on the combined organizational and administrative environment; the other five environments are treated in other chapters of this volume.

Environmental domain refers to a subset of an environment, which includes similar sets of organizational variables. It is useful to subdivide the organizational and administrative environment into five major conceptual domains that can influence faculty teaching and, either directly or indirectly, student learning outcomes. These five domains are organizational strategy, academic management practices, organizational culture, and two types of organizational climate: the perceived organizational climate, and the felt, or psychological, climate of the organization. Each of these domains within the organizational and administrative environment will be discussed in terms of its potential relationship to student learning outcomes. (It is important to note here that these domains also may influence other categories of institutional effectiveness and functional outcomes, in addition to the teaching and learning function of institutions, but those others are beyond the scope of this chapter.)

In the discussion that follows, many institutional characteristics—such as size, control, complexity, and type of institution, extent of teaching emphasis, and nature of the student clientele—may moderate or enhance not only learning outcomes but also the impacts of various sets of organizational variables or domains. For example, we know that many of these domains may be more influential in small residential colleges. Thus, the appropriateness of each domain is to some extent dependent on its larger institutional context. In the sections that follow, I will comment on each domain briefly in terms of its nature, why it is important, and how it might affect teaching and student learning. Discussion of these domains begins with those that are broad and moves toward those that are more specific, but this order does not imply a causal direction; obviously, organizational and administrative patterns may either affect teaching and learning behavior or emerge from it.

Organizational Strategy. The first useful domain of the organizational and administrative environment is the organization's academic strategy, which gives a sense of direction and purpose to college and university academic and educational activities. This domain might be termed the *academic guidance function* of an institution. Strategy may be defined and examined in terms of the institution's stated formal mission and purposes, the "fit" of the internal environments and functional patterns with the press of external environments or major constituents, and the broad patterns of organizational structure and function present in an institution. In a sense, all of these definitions can be reflected along a number of common conceptual and content dimensions. Some major conceptual dimensions of strategy (and their subsets) reflected in the literature are the following (Peterson, 1980).

1. *Nature or purpose.* Does the institution emphasize a strategic approach, which attempts to relate the institution to changing external environmental conditions? an interpretive approach, in which emphasis is placed on conveying and interpreting the institution's mission through its values, symbols, and traditions? a managerial approach, in which a rational hierarchy of goals is defined and stressed? an entrepreneurial approach, which stimulates innovative and even risky ventures? or a contingency approach, which develops strategies for possible future problems, constraints, or opportunities?

2. *Internal or external orientation.* Does the institutional strategy focus primarily on internal phenomena, making the institution more efficient or effective at what it is currently doing, or does it focus on external environmental changes and ways the institution should respond?

3. *Source of control.* Who controls the institution's future? Is it primarily assumed that the institution controls its own future, or that it

is externally controlled? Can the organization be proactive and shape external conditions? Does it anticipate environmental changes and attempt to adapt its strategy to the most supportive external changes? Does it merely respond to changes as they occur? Or does it only react to external changes after the fact (or even resist)?

4. *Competitive orientation.* Does the institution seek cooperative relationships with other educational institutions and agencies, or does it adopt a competitive stance?

5. *Future orientation.* Does the institutional strategy take a short- or long-term view of its mission and goals?

6. *Change orientation.* Does the institution have a particular approach to institutional change to accomplish its mission and goals? Is the approach rationally planned, managerially directed or mandated, or opportunistic? Is the time frame short or long?

7. *Organization-member relationship.* Does the institution's strategy and change orientation assume that the organization has a good deal of control over members' behavior, or does it recognize, tolerate, or encourage significant flexibility?

8. *Mission and goal orientation.* To what degree are mission and goals formally or informally emphasized or made explicit? Are they clear and consistent?

9. *Consistency.* Is there consistency among the different elements of an institution's strategy?

10. *Consensus.* Are important constituent groups in agreement regarding an institution's strategy and its various elements?

11. *Legitimacy.* Do the major constituents agree that their strategy has been legitimately developed and is in the best interests of the institution? Are they willing to participate and contribute?

While all these dimensions of the academic strategy domain are conceptually interesting, higher education research suggests that three dimensions have been particularly useful to institutions trying to recover from enrollment decline or attempting to redirect their educational purposes or programs: emphasizing strategic and interpretive planning approaches concurrently (the institution-environment fit and how institutional leadership employs symbolic behavior to influence direction), focusing on mission and goal clarity, and using strategies that are consistent and legitimate in the eyes of institutional participants (Zammuto, 1987). Institutions do attempt to devise academic strategies and to guide their direction in various ways, but it is also important to study, more specifically than has been the case, how these dimensions influence teaching and learning behaviors over time.

While an institution's academic strategy can be viewed along conceptual dimensions in a number of ways (Chaffee, 1985), it also is important to examine the content dimensions. A number of content dimensions along which strategy has been examined can be identified in most institutional settings. They include the following:

- Academic planning emphasis
- Mission and goal content (teaching approach, learning mode, or outcome emphasis; clientele; educational orientation; program mix; service region)
- Style of academic governance (decision process, participation pattern, and so on)
- Administrative leadership (decision style, educational supportiveness, academic legitimacy, consistency, and so on)
- Symbolic emphasis on undergraduate education
- Academic administrative structure (priority or status of undergraduate educational administration and coordination)
- Academic or educational resource allocation priority.

Institutions, or major units within them, vary along the eleven conceptual and seven content dimensions of organizational academic strategy. Many of the dimensions are varied intentionally, in an attempt to influence the institution's academic image or direction, teaching behavior, or student learning. Examining institutional strategy is often complex, but focusing on strategy and its dimensions is important for at least five reasons. First, the strategy domain consists of variables that can be manipulated to redirect institutional effort. Second, it may establish an important academic climate. Third, it can and should provide direction for implementing consistent academic management practices to reinforce academic climate. Fourth, to the extent that an institution wants to influence its culture, emphasizing strategic dimensions over time may be useful. Finally, strategy that provides a strong sense of direction and stability assists institutions in struggling against uncertainty or attempting to redirect academic emphasis.

Academic Management Practices. A second major domain of the organizational and administrative environment, these are defined as the formally organized activities, policies, and procedures that an institution explicitly devises to implement its educational strategy and to support teaching and learning. This domain, concerned with how the institution supports teaching and learning, is important for at least three reasons. First, although faculty and academic administrators regularly establish organizational and administrative practices specifically to support teaching and learning, few of these practices have been examined to assess their actual impact. For example, faculty development activities have been evaluated in terms of their impact on faculty roles, attitudes, and behaviors, but apparently not in terms of changes in student learning. Second, the fit between formal practices and individuals' perceptions of their supportiveness may be very poor; thus, these practices are rendered ineffective, even when well intentioned. Third, since considerable staff effort and resources can be invested in academic management activities, it is important to know if different patterns or combinations (for example, practices that are faculty-focused or student-focused) or different approaches (incentives versus mandated policies) will work most effectively to improve faculty teaching and to encourage student learning efforts.

Again, there are many ways to categorize the numerous academic management practices that institutions have introduced in order to improve teaching and learning. For example, in a recent open-ended survey of three hundred "scholar-administrators" (campus chief executive officers who have published or given major presentations on improving undergraduate education), respondents mentioned over two hundred practices that they felt enhanced an emphasis on teaching and on student learning on their campuses (Peterson, Cameron, Mets, and others, 1987). Such practices can be categorized in terms of both substantive content and conceptual dimensions. In addition to the content of an institution's academic strategy, previously discussed, content grouping of academic management practices might include those related to the following areas:

- Academic information, analysis, and feedback systems
- Academic resource allocation
- Admissions and enrollment management
- Academic, curriculum, and program policy
- Program review and development
- Utilization of educational technology and computers
- Instructional and teaching improvement
- Faculty recruitment, selection, and promotion
- Faculty development
- Faculty evaluation and assessment
- Faculty rewards and incentives
- Student academic support services
- Student assessment.

Since people on campuses generally perceive the management practices included in these categories as important, extensive changes in them are taking place at many institutions. In the public sector, many such changes are initiated at the state level. Such practices as student assessment, incentive funding for educational excellence and improvement, program review, and targeted instructional support are now frequently endorsed.

Along conceptual dimensions, it is also possible to examine the pattern of institutional academic management practices on such important dimensions as breadth or comprehensiveness of available practices, focus of the practices (faculty, student, curriculum, and so on), accessibility and supportiveness, educational emphasis or orientation (focus on teaching or learning), control or incentive orientation for student or faculty involvement, and consistency among practices.

In examining academic management practices, it seems important to understand the extent and nature of these developments on any campus, the conceptual patterns that are emerging, and the resources expended on the various practices, as well as to assess which practices appear to be most useful or effective. While management practices may directly or indirectly influence the teaching and learning climate, the ultimate concern is whether they influence student learning.

Organizational Culture. The two conceptual domains of organizational culture and organizational climate can constructively be conceived as distinct, and thus we will consider each one briefly. *Organizational culture* means the values, beliefs, or ideologies that participants share about their institutions. Culture is the domain that provides participants with a personal sense of meaning for institutional purposes and that reinforces their own sense of belonging; in an educational institution, it could be considered the academic "glue." Compared to climate, culture is focused on relatively few major content dimensions that have crucial meaning for participants, are deeply embedded in organizational life, have continuity over time, and give participants a sense that their institution is distinctive. Clark's (1970) landmark study of Antioch, Reed, and Swarthmore confirmed the importance of culture and the difficulty of changing it. A growing research literature (Dill, 1982) continues to examine the existence and importance of culture in higher education. Clearly, some institutions have strong cultures, attract certain types of students and faculty, perpetuate the culture, and have powerful influences on their graduates.

Studying culture is difficult because culture is, by definition, what makes an institution or its members feel (correctly or not) unique or distinctive. It is difficult to identify any uniform dimensions of culture to analyze. Culture can be measured in numerous ways (surveys, interviews, observation, content analysis) and focused on diverse phenomena (member perceptions, observed patterns of behavior, symbolic behavior, institutional history or traditions). Examples of broad content areas into which studies of educationally relevant aspects of an institution's culture seem to fall include the role of the institution in society, the institution's educational mission or goal, its governance philosophy, its educational philosophy or emphasis on a particular mode of learning, and the intellectual orientation of its students.

While the content of an institution's academic culture may exemplify how people perceive the institution's purpose, culture itself may vary along a number of conceptual dimensions that are useful for examining the relationship of academic culture to teaching and learning behavior. Conceptual dimensions along which culture can be examined include institutional distinctiveness of culture, continuity of culture over time, embeddedness of culture in all aspects of organizational life, strength of culture (in terms of control over member behavior), congruence among elements of the culture, degree of cultural consensus among members, clarity of cultural focus, and type of cultural content.

Clearly, the more closely attuned the content of an institution's culture is to teaching and learning, the more crucial it becomes. Since the strength of an institution's culture may vary, and because culture is usually difficult to change, it may serve different purposes in different institutions.

To cite the importance of culture in any organizational discussion is to recognize that climate and culture probably overlap—that culture may influence climate or even be more powerful than climate in affecting teaching and learning behavior, but that culture is also more difficult to change. In one institution, culture may be an important domain to create or strengthen, in order to instill a desired teaching or learning orientation. In another institution, a strong culture that attracts and motivates people may be useful to reinforce. Where culture does not serve the institution's educational purpose, a long-term strategy may be required to change it.

Organizational Climate. Although the terms *climate* and *culture* overlap and often are used interchangeably, the two can be usefully distinguished if we define *climate* as the current organizational patterns of important dimensions of organizational life, together with members' perceptions and attitudes toward them. This distinction allows us to examine climate, in comparison to culture, as an embedded style or content-specific atmosphere.

Three broad types or definitions of climate can be identified. These focus on somewhat different (if overlapping) phenomena. *Objective climate* focuses on the observable patterns of behavior or formal activity in an institution. For example, patterns in the domain of academic management practices could be described as the objective climate of an institution. *Perceived climate* includes images that participants hold of how organizational life does and should function. These perceptions, accurate or not, may shape norms that support or discourage behavior. *Psychological, or felt, climate* is the motivational dimension: how participants feel about their organization, including their loyalty and commitment to it, their morale, their beliefs about their quality of effort, and their sense of belonging. A variety of conceptual and content dimensions are important in examining perceived and psychological climate. The following is a partial list of conceptual dimensions that have appeared in studies assessing climate.

- Differentiation among institutions or subgroups
- Limited continuity
- Strength (control over individual members' behavior)
- Congruence among content elements around which climate is examined

- Consensus among members or subgroups who perceive climate
- Clarity of focus
- Supportiveness
- Importance or salience to those perceiving climate
- Type (content elements) of climate.

While these conceptual dimensions of climate clearly overlap with dimensions of culture, climate has limited continuity. It does not emphasize embeddedness and institutional distinctiveness; in fact, common content may be used to differentiate institutional climates. It may include many content elements, rather than the few broad, intensively held beliefs or values that are the core of culture. Examples of broad content categories of perceived academic climate include the faculty's and administrators' perceptions of many of the following areas of organizational life.

- Academic strategy and academic management practices (see earlier discussion for categories)
- Patterns of governance and leadership
- Academic work environment (especially for faculty)
- Academic change
- Institutional functioning
- Educational climate
- Teaching and learning orientation
- Views of other environments (student, curricular, educational technology, or external).

Both the perceived climate and the psychological climate are amenable to quantitative survey measurement and have been used to distinguish among institutions, among subgroups of students, faculty, and administrators, and among participants in different organizational units. However, there is relatively little evidence to link either the perceived or psychological domains of climate to learning outcomes.

The content of psychological climate differs, by definition, from that of perceived climate, and this distinction may be useful, for several reasons. First, the felt climate indicators (such as motivation, loyalty, commitment) have been useful predictors of performance in many organizational settings. In higher education, they have been found to be related to faculty performance.

Second, given the difficulty of measuring student learning outcomes, psychological climate may be useful when viewed as a dependent variable for faculty and academic administrators and as an important intervening variable among the various organizational domain variables and learning outcomes (see Figure 2).

Third, most of the climate research in higher education has been on perceived climate. Commonly used examples include the *Institutional Goals Inventory, Institutional Functioning Inventory, Student Reactions to College* (all from Educational Testing Service), and other commercially

Figure 2. The Academic Organizational Context

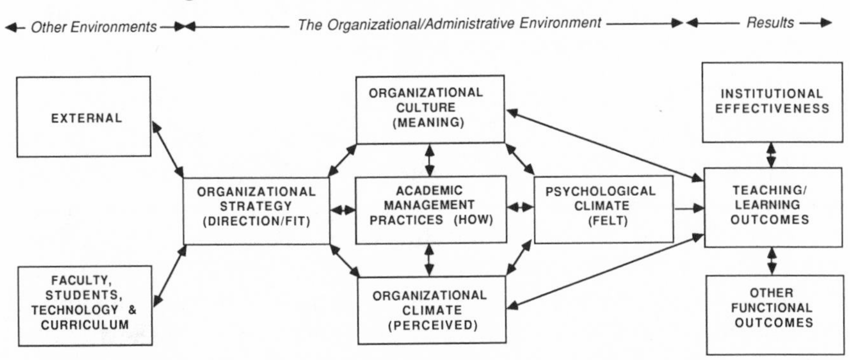

available instruments. While these instruments may be useful in distinguishing among institutions, most have not been very helpful in predicting such specific institutional outcomes as student learning. One possible explanation may be that these instruments have focused on general patterns of organizational life, rather than relating specifically to educational processes, faculty teaching, and student learning behavior. In the case of our organizational framework, for example, existing instruments have not focused on strategic or academic management practices that have been designed explicitly to support teaching and learning behaviors. Clearly, perceived climate measures that focus on the availability, utility, and supportiveness of various strategic domain patterns and academic management practices might be useful predictors of faculty psychological climate, student climate, or even student learning. That usefulness, however, remains hypothetical.

Fourth, research on student climate has been somewhat useful in predicting student attitude change, student retention, and even longer-term behavioral change. However, even this literature has been relatively ineffective in terms of predicting student learning.

Measures of perceived academic climate may yet be useful if conceptualized and applied somewhat differently. They should focus to a greater degree than has been true on the perceptions and feelings of faculty and academic administrators, rather than on perceptions of students. Faculty and administrators are the individuals who must be motivated to improve teaching and to focus on student learning needs or concerns. They are also the most enduring institutional members and thus can be most directly influenced by organizational strategy or changes in those academic management practices designed intentionally to improve teaching and learning. Moreover, perceived climate may be an important variable if measures focus on the elements of organizational life directly designed to support teaching and learning. Some plausible content dimensions reflecting faculty members' and academic administrators' perceptions of climate may be in the domains of strategy and academic management practices, previously discussed. Standardized instruments for measuring climate perceptions in this domain do not currently exist.

An Agenda for Scholars and Institutional Researchers

I have presented this framework as a guide for examining five domains in the organizational and administrative environment. Each domain has several dimensions and thus suggests a broad array of variables that may have important effects on the institutional teaching and learning climate. Therefore, each domain may directly or indirectly influence student learning and is open to study by institutional researchers. It is clear that these environmental variables are farther removed from the activity of learning than are variables directly related to curriculum and teaching. Nevertheless, the dimensions of academic strategy and academic management practices are variables that administrators and faculty groups can and do use in attempts to influence climate (and possibly culture) and thus directly or indirectly to improve teaching and student learning.

While we continue, intuitively, to believe that these strategic and academic management practices are important, we have little firm evidence to link them to student learning. Thus, not only do we have a set of important research questions for evaluating how strategy and academic management practices influence climate and student learning, we also face a set of broader issues relevant to both scholarly and institutional research. These include the following.

1. Given the intuitive importance of (but unimpressive evidence concerning) the impact of organizational and administrative environment variables on student learning, how much effort should we direct to evaluating such variables, as compared to the direct impact of classroom, curricular, faculty, teaching, or student behavior variables? More important, can we find out which variables have greatest influence?

2. Given the limited resources of most institutions, how much should we invest in improved academic management practices, and with what priority? This question clearly suggests evaluation research to determine which academic management and support service activities most usefully affect an institution's teaching and learning climate and its student learning outcomes.

3. To what extent should institutional strategy be emphasized in order to change institutional culture? Difficult changes in culture may be necessary to introduce major academic redirection or improvement of teaching and learning. Should we focus on strategies to change culture, or should we focus on academic management practices and attempt to change climate, while allowing culture to evolve over the long term?

4. If the academic strategy and academic management practice dimensions are primary variables of importance, how do institutions ensure the involvement of faculty and the full range of academic administrators to avoid a top-down sense of redirection, which may undermine many intentionally designed efforts to improve the teaching and learning climate or student learning itself?

5. According to research evidence, in small institutions or in subunits of large ones, institutional mission, leadership, culture, and climate have the greatest impact on full-time students and faculty. Are these domains therefore less critical in the large, diffuse institutions that enroll the majority of our students? Also, in large institutions, what is the appropriate subunit (school or department) to which an organizational and administrative analysis should be applied and in which research should be carried out?

The Institutional Researcher: Monitor, Evaluator, and Scholarly Collaborator

We know intuitively that domains in the organizational and administrative environment make a difference. On the basis of this knowledge and the previous research framework for such explorations, we can discover at least three key roles for institutional researchers.

The first is a broad monitoring role. Student learning outcomes and the perceived psychological climates of faculty and academic administrators are variables that institutional researchers can monitor, using an initial diagnosis of the institution's emphasis on teaching and learning performance. Even more practically, distinctions between strategies and patterns of practices and faculty perception of them may be useful in diagnosing problem areas. Finally, it might help to determine if changes in the institution's strategy or academic management practices produced desired effects. Such effects may be observed in faculty perceptions of the organizational and administrative environment's supportiveness for teaching and learning, their own involvement in and commitment to teaching and student learning, and the measured student learning that takes place. Institutional researchers are beginning to give more attention to such a monitoring role in light of recent national reports, state-level actions, pressures from accreditation agencies, and institutional concerns about the quality of education.

Beyond providing descriptive institutional evaluation, institutional researchers can also evaluate which dimensions or elements of strategy or academic management practices have desired effects on climate and student learning. This second, evaluative role suggests both focused program reviews and studies that examine specific elements of strategy and specific practices, as well as broad assessments of an entire institution's academic management strategy and patterns of academic management practices. The prospect of assessing broad patterns requires some institutionwide criteria for these domains, which might include the following:

- The nature of academic strategy (planning and goal emphasis)
- The institutional priority or emphasis on teaching and learning (academic structure)
- Resource priority (symbolic support)
- Leadership support
- Breadth or comprehensiveness of organizational commitment to academic management practices
- Supportiveness or availability of academic management practices
- Balance of focus of academic management practices (students, faculty, instruction, curriculum)
- Emphasis of practices (student- or faculty-oriented? selection-, development-, improvement-, or evaluation-oriented? control- or incentive-oriented?)
- Consistency among practices.

While this discussion has suggested a strong evaluation role for institutional researchers in monitoring and examining the educational impacts of organizational and administrative patterns and practices, it also suggests studies involving multiple institutions. It is important to understand how organizational and administrative patterns (as well as faculty, curricular, and classroom patterns) influence student learning. In order to contribute to that understanding, institutional researchers attempting to assess educational effectiveness may wish to participate in interinstitutional research programs. Such programs may be devised by institutional researchers with common interests, or in collaboration with research scholars interested in comprehensive studies.

Understanding the impact of organizational and administrative variables on student learning can provide us with an excellent opportunity to learn more about colleges and universities—not just as economic, collegial, managerial, or political organizations, but also as organizations devised to deliver educational services. The ultimate test of an appropriate role for institutional research is the measurement of impact on academic culture, the teaching and learning climate, and student learning.

References

Bowen, H. R. *Investment in Learning: The Individual and Social Value of American Higher Education.* San Francisco: Jossey-Bass, 1977.

Chaffee, E. E. "The Concept of Strategy: From Business to Higher Education." In J. S. Smart (ed.), *Higher Education: Handbook of Theory and Research.* Vol. 1. New York: Agathon, 1985.

Clark, B. R. *The Distinctive College: Antioch, Reed, and Swarthmore.* Chicago: Aldine, 1970.

Dill, D. D. "The Management of Academic Culture: Notes on the Management of Meaning and Social Integration." *Higher Education,* 1982, *11,* 303–320.

Pascarella, E. T. "College Environmental Influences on Learning and Cognitive Development: A Critical Review and Synthesis." In J. S. Smart (ed.), *Higher Education: Handbook of Theory and Research.* Vol. 1. New York: Agathon, 1985.

Peterson, M. W. "Analyzing Alternative Approaches to Planning." In P. Jedamus, M. W. Peterson, and Associates, *Improving Academic Management: A Handbook of Planning and Institutional Research.* San Francisco: Jossey-Bass, 1980.

Peterson, M. W., Cameron, K. S., Alexander, J., Jones, P., and Mets, L. A. *Key Problems Inhibiting the Improvement of Teaching and Learning.* Ann Arbor: National Center for Research to Improve Postsecondary Teaching and Learning, University of Michigan, 1987.

Peterson, M. W., Cameron, K. S., Mets, L. A., Jones, P., and Ettington, D. *The Organizational Context for Teaching and Learning: A Review of the Literature.* Ann Arbor: National Center for Research to Improve Postsecondary Teaching and Learning, University of Michigan, 1986.

Peterson, M. W., Cameron, K. S., Mets, L. A., Jones, P., and Ettington, D. *Executive Summary: The Organizational Context for Teaching and Learning.* Ann Arbor: National Center for Research to Improve Postsecondary Teaching and Learning, University of Michigan, 1987.

Smart, J. C., and Montgomery, J. (eds.). *Examining Departmental Management.* New Directions for Institutional Research, no. 10. San Francisco: Jossey-Bass, 1976.

Zammuto, R. F. "Managing Declining Enrollments and Revenues." In M. W. Peterson and L. A. Mets (eds.), *Key Resources on Higher Education Governance, Management, and Leadership: A Guide to the Literature.* San Francisco: Jossey-Bass, 1987.

Marvin W. Peterson is director of the Center for the Study of Higher and Postsecondary Education, professor in the Program on Higher and Adult Continuing Education, and research program director in the National Center for Research to Improve Postsecondary Teaching and Learning (NCRIPTAL), at the University of Michigan.

Viewing curriculum as an academic plan permits development of parallel course and program planning models that are dynamic, conceptually related to student learning, and familiar to institutional planners.

Perspectives on Course and Program Planning

Joan S. Stark, Malcolm A. Lowther

During the next decade, an important research question to be answered is: Does the way college courses and programs are designed affect student learning? Currently, colleges are receptive to curricular experimentation that holds promise for improving student learning outcomes. Consequently, an old definition of institutional research as the "activity in which the mission orientation and the discipline orientation of a college or university intersect" (Dyer, 1966) may again apply, as faculty and institutional research offices become partners.

If the "responsibility of the faculty as a whole for the curriculum as a whole" can be revived (Association of American Colleges, 1985), departmental faculties may seek answers to pressing questions about student outcomes. In a context of strong and often conflicting faculty value systems among departments, institutional researchers may help to ensure that research questions are neutral, that interpretations of data are objective and practical, and that evaluation of newly implemented policies is planned. Even if institutional researchers are not invited by disciplinary specialists to assist with such assessments, they may nevertheless be involved through external demands for documentation of institutional success. Thus, although roles of institutional researchers in exploring and measuring undergraduate curriculum effectiveness may vary from

J. S. Stark and L. A. Mets (eds.). *Improving Teaching and Learning Through Research.*
New Directions for Institutional Research, no. 57. San Francisco: Jossey-Bass, Spring 1988.

college to college, most will need potentially useful models to help guide research or to interpret new information.

Curriculum Literature Not Too Helpful

The institutional researcher interested in the college curriculum will find a vast array of general literature. For example, in selecting readings potentially relevant to faculty curriculum committee members, at least thirteen categories of literature are identifiable (see Table 1). Unfortunately for the researcher, much of this literature is historical, anecdotal, or rhetorically prescriptive and yields few frameworks to guide analysis of college course impacts on students (Conrad and Pratt, 1986; Stark and Lowther, 1986). Frequently, articles and books begin with premises about what an educated person should know, and they go on to argue with weak evidence that certain processes will lead to acquisition of this knowledge. Such descriptive essays, rather than analytic treatments, seem to be the most common form of curricular discussion (Toombs, 1977-78).

In the current charged climate of educational reform, the persuasive arguments of those whose educational preferences are endangered may appear with increasing frequency. For example, while enrollments burgeon in professional or occupational programs, many academics advocate with increased fervor the values of undergraduate liberal study. While new instruments are being demanded and developed to measure student

Table 1. Types of Literature Bearing on the Postsecondary Curriculum

1. Social and economic needs and trends related to higher education
2. Debates and advocacy positions regarding educational goals
3. Historical traditions and perspectives
4. Reports on current curriculum designs and change trends
5. Studies of student characteristics and learning styles
6. Guidebooks and handbooks on counseling and advising
7. Techniques of measuring student outcomes
8. Teaching styles and strategies
9. Instructional resources and tools
10. Faculty evaluation
11. Change processes
12. Program evaluation and long-range planning
13. Relation of educational goals and discipline structure to course and program design

outcomes, critics of testing renew accusations of bias. Such ideological debates are difficult to resolve and may have contributed to the paucity, reported in a recent review, of empirical work connecting curricular elements and student cognitive outcomes (Pascarella, 1985). Recently, however, relatively comprehensive research models on curriculum outcomes have emerged in work done at Alverno College and several other colleges (Mentkowski and Doherty, 1984; Winter, McClelland, and Stewart, 1982). Although the emergence of such models responds to the need for systematic ways to explore and improve the postsecondary curriculum, little progress has been made toward developing grounded curriculum theories to guide studies in higher education (Dressel, 1980; Toombs, 1977-78).

Essential to systematic data collection, as well as to any emergent model or theory, is clarity regarding the level of analysis at which curriculum effectiveness should be examined. Some speculate that efforts to document curricular effects on student learning have failed because, while educational impact is felt in programs and departments, outcome measures have been aggregated at the institutional level (Pascarella, 1985; Ewell, 1984). Although our review is incomplete, we find that educational research at the program level, sometimes found in journals of the academic disciplines, is sparse and lacks sophistication and meaningful synthesis. Thus, although the need for curriculum change underlies all recent national critiques of higher education, there is little firm ground on which to build. Lacking both evidence and models, the public has every reason to be skeptical about the stewardship colleges have exercised over student intellectual growth. The current period of emphasis on assessment of educational quality seems to portend a shift in research from descriptive, anecdotal, and polemical statements about curriculum to data-based studies.

The Importance of Defining Curriculum

The trend toward more empirical curriculum studies is fostered by federal project sponsorship (Office of Educational Research and Improvement, 1986), state initiatives (Boyer and McGuinness, 1986), and institutional publicity (Northeast Missouri State University, 1984). Yet this shift is based on a widely disseminated reform literature, in which the ambiguous term *curriculum* is frequently modified by several equally ambiguous adjectives (such as *coherent* and *rigorous*) or by such undefined processes as *integration*. One reason why the literature on postsecondary curriculum is rooted more in rhetoric than in research is that the concept of postsecondary curriculum is diffuse and its definition imprecise. The term *curriculum* may mean (1) the college's or program's mission or collective expression of what is important for students to learn, (2) a set of experiences that some authorities believe all students should have, (3) a set of courses offered to students, (4) a set of courses students actually elect from those available, (5) the content of a specific discipline, and (6) the time and credit frame in which a college provides education. As a consequence of these varying definitions, any writer or researcher is free to proceed as if curriculum were a purpose, a process, or a product.

Thus, even among knowledgeable individuals, a discussion of curriculum changes can focus on changes in college goals, on mechanistic changes in curricular support processes (such as the college calendar or credit system), or on substantive changes (such as the realignment of academic fields or educational outcomes expected of students). By some accounts, campus discussions focusing on mechanical changes and routines receive more attention than substantive discussions (Bergquist, Gould, and Greenberg, 1981). Such emphases may help to explain the lack of substantive models of curricular change and the low regard in which some hold curricular research. It is therefore appropriate to clarify concepts so that a systematic body of knowledge about curriculum, curricular change, and curricular effects can be generated.

To establish a starting point for cumulative empirical studies of curriculum-related issues, we have built on the work of others (Taba, 1962; Toombs, 1977-78; Gay, 1980) to define *curriculum* as *an academic plan* embodied in a course or a program of courses and implying the following elements.

1. A selection of knowledge, skills, and attitudes to be learned related to desired educational goals or purposes
2. A selection of subject matter in which to embed educational activities directed at acquiring those knowledge, skills, and attitudes
3. A consideration of the learners' previous backgrounds and skills
4. A design for the educational activities, including sequencing of materials
5. A selection of materials, sources, tools, and settings to foster learning
6. A method for evaluating student learning
7. A system for considering and revising items 1 through 5 in light of the result of item 6.

This definition includes the major variables that typically surface when planning, implementing, evaluating, or improving teaching and learning are discussed. Thus, the concept of curriculum as a plan provides a suitable umbrella under which the many disparate literatures treating teaching and learning can be interrelated. Unlike the static definition of curriculum as a set of courses, which has not guided comprehensive change, this dynamic planning definition should be attractive to policymakers, for its built-in feedback mechanism encourages interactive change and improvement.

The definition allows institutional-level researchers and planners to extrapolate and adapt familiar analytic techniques to program and classroom settings. The definition also may appeal to faculty members knowledgeable about design processes in fields as diverse as art, writing, and engineering (Toombs, 1977–78). Since nothing about the definition specifies teaching content or style, even instructors who view all or most educational planning models as excessively mechanistic may recognize that their own flexible academic plans fit under the umbrella. Finally, viewing curriculum as an academic plan for individual students and groups of students disaggregates the fundamental nature of the educational process. It emphasizes that the primary goal of the institution is to devote thoughtful attention to promoting student learning.

Opportunities Gained by Using the Academic Plan Umbrella for Curriculum

Beyond its fundamental nature, flexibility, and familiarity, the definition of curriculum as an academic plan highlights other important opportunities. We will discuss several such opportunities in light of research now in progress.

Opportunity 1: Identification of Influences on Educational Planning

When the curriculum is conceptualized as a plan, a variety of factors and potential influences on its design can be readily identified, assessed, and even experimentally varied. Viewing the curriculum as an academic plan allows us to identify and study the strength of various influences on faculty planning. For example, on the basis of an extensive literature review (Stark and Lowther, 1986), a tentative model of course planning can be built based on the work of others (Phenix, 1964; Dressel and Marcus, 1982; Clark and Peterson, 1986; Schwab, 1964; Posner and Rudnitsky, 1982; Confrey, 1981; King and Brownell, 1966). *Course planning* can be defined as the decision-making process in which instructors select content to be taught, consider various factors affecting the teaching and learning process, and choose from among alternative strategies for engaging students with the content. Planning also includes the selection of methods to obtain feedback about student learning in order to improve the decision-making process in the future.

To verify the elements tentatively included in the planning model, we explored influences on planning of introductory courses through interviews with eighty-nine faculty members representing eight fields in five different types of colleges. The specific sets of influences we explored are listed in the left-hand column, "Course Design Influences," of Table 2.

Table 2. Parallel Models of Course and Program Planning

Course Design Influences	Program Design Influences
Course Design Influences	*Program Design Influences*
Discipline characteristics	Discipline characteristics
	Institutional characteristics
Faculty characteristics	Program characteristics
Background	Faculty mix
Educational assumptions	Educational assumptions
Observed student characteristics	Observed student characteristics
Program goals	
College goals	College goals
Input from other sources	Input from other sources
External sources (includes textbooks)	External sources
On-campus sources	On-campus sources (includes governance and budget allocation
Internal sources (includes feedback from student evaluation	Internal sources (includes resources and political factors)
Expert opinion	Expert opinion
Other pressures, influences, or resources	Other pressures, influences, or resources
Course Design Components	*Program Design Components*
Course objectives	Program objectives
Sequencing of content	Program coherence
Instructional mode	Program implementation

Although data analysis is incomplete, some early observations may be useful for institutional researchers.

- Faculty participate cheerfully and, by their reports, profitably, in interviews about course planning.
- Among the strongest influences on course planning are the academic field and faculty perceptions of student characteristics.
- Faculty members plan differently for introductory-level courses than for more advanced courses.
- Except in professional fields where specialized accreditation is a factor, and at community colleges with stringent four-year college articulation agreements, relatively few factors external to the college influence faculty course planning.
- Some influences (for example, institutional mission and program goals) either are unimportant or faculty members are not conscious of their effects.
- The availability of resources and facilities is seen as a potent influence on course planning if resources are lacking but lacks influence if no deficits are apparent.

- Faculty seldom mention service offices on campus (student services, instructional development, library, testing office, and so on) as useful or relevant in course planning. The exceptions are student assistance centers for tutoring, drill, or practice.
- Although faculty believe student characteristics are important, they generally do not receive related data before a course begins.
- Faculty frequently mention student evaluations from previous classes as useful for course revision.

As these early general findings illustrate, if salient influences on faculty course planning on one's own campus can be discovered, institutional researchers may go beyond outcome assessment to identify ways to assist faculty in improving education. What is perhaps most important, defining curriculum as a plan at the course level permits us to examine, across settings, variations in four important factors affecting the learning process: the field of study (content), the type of institution (context), the instructional plan (form), and the type of student for whom the plan is intended (client) (Stark and Lowther, 1986).

Opportunity 2: Consistent Planning Models

The definition of curriculum as a plan allows parallel planning models constructed at several organizational levels to be examined for utility and consistency. Whether or not one views academic specialties as culprits in fragmenting the curriculum (Association of American Colleges, 1985), disciplines and professions have become the organizers of our knowledge, history, and experience (Dressel and Marcus, 1982). They possess varied epistemologies and characteristic theories, which consistently influence the content of individual courses (Confrey, 1981). In the aggregate, the goals of organized groups of faculty (departments, divisions, programs) reflect these disciplinary characteristics, although they are mediated by institutional realities. At a broader level, the college's mission is typically more encompassing in scope, while the goals of students are more individualized.

Viewing curriculum as an academic plan permits study of why and how individuals and groups at these several levels establish and implement educational goals. Thus, academic plans may be prepared by faculty members for their classes of students (course plans), by individual students and their advisers for their personalized education (advisement plans), by groups of faculty members for programs under their supervision (academic program plans), and by college or university officials to carry out the institutional mission (institutional plan).

Table 2 shows lists of parallel influences that we assume may affect educational planning at the course and program levels. In our view, one previously unexplored analogy in these two lists not only serves to explain the utility of the parallelism but may have particular heuristic value. This is the construct of arranging or sequencing material in specific courses (Posner and Rudnitsky, 1982). To illustrate, we may relate faculty members' views of planned arrangements for course content to their disciplines, educational beliefs, and external influences. Similarly, at the program level, the preferred sequencing of course units in the academic program plan (or in the individual advisement plan) is based on similar sets of influences. Identifying the strength of these influences can illuminate realities that limit the definition and implementation of widely discussed ideals, such as curricular coherence or integrity. Thus, just as course content may be arranged so as to expose students to increasingly difficult concepts, build their cumulative knowledge base, and relate ideas from one discipline to those of other disciplines or to societal issues, it can be argued that the combination of courses faculty specify as constituting coherent student programs might be examined along such dimensions as hierarchy, prescriptiveness, and interrelatedness. The planning model allows exploration of whether this analogy holds, or whether in program planning (as some might claim) political trade-offs and territorial rights within and between groups of faculty are more influential than educational beliefs.

Opportunity 3: Cognitive Integration and Curricular Coherence

The integration implied in a curriculum plan can be linked with psychological theories of cognitive integration, to view learning as reconstructing knowledge when new information is meshed with old. The concepts of coherence and integration, inherent in viewing curriculum as an academic plan, are useful in another sense as well. Recent research in cognitive psychology holds strong potential for improving educational practice. Cognitive psychologists suggest that learners are engaged actively in the construction of knowledge by developing knowledge structures to assist them in comprehending the meaning of knowledge and acquiring new knowledge. For instructional practice, such suggestions imply that students can learn how to learn (see Chapter Five) and that learning can be viewed as the product of interaction between events in the educational environment and in students' internal cognitive processing systems. In other words, successful academic functioning—the achievement of desired outcomes—results from a combination of sound cognitive functioning and appropriately chosen educational content and activities.

Course revision (or, at the program level, curricular revision) can no longer simply be an exercise in upgrading content, just as teaching cannot be merely the transmission of content from expert to novice. To facilitate meaningful knowledge acquisition, the curriculum planner must arrange the material in ways that facilitate its incorporation into the student's existing knowledge structure. Since one meaning of the popular term *curricular coherence* suggests deliberate and planned attention to the conceptual interrelatedness of material within and between fields of study, such strategies as describing the teacher's conceptual map of the discipline to students, and sequencing course content to help the student organize and assimilate new ideas, may take on new importance.

Opportunity 4: Expectations, Feedback, and Student Involvement

Defining curriculum as an academic plan can make concrete some ideas believed important in improving collegiate learning: setting clear expectations for students, providing students with feedback, and fostering student involvement.

Setting Expectations for Students. According to one national report, restoring excellence to higher education requires that "demonstrable improvements in student knowledge, capacities, skills, and attitudes" occur "within established, clearly expressed and publicly announced and maintained standards of performance" (NIE Study Group, 1984, p. 15). Subsequent discussion has centered on ways of demonstrating improvements in student knowledge; there has been less discussion of the possible role that establishing standards or clarifying expectations may play in increasing achievement. One good reason for viewing curriculum as a plan is to ensure inclusion of such key elements as purposes, the means to accomplish the purposes, and expectations or criteria for success. It follows that educational improvement should result from a deliberate change in some element of the plan, rather than from the mere act of measuring whether criteria are achieved. Indeed, the forms of communicating expectations to students can be identified as a specific element in the plan. What is most appealing to the researcher, the communication methods can be readily varied to determine whether clarity of course and program objectives affects learning outcomes.

In our exploratory interviews with faculty members, we found that most were able to articulate goals for their students. They frequently described these goals and expectations in a course syllabus and discussed them explicitly with students early in their courses. They reported using many other creative ways of communicating expectations to students throughout the term. Unfortunately, however, not all instructors felt confident that each student received the messages or understood the expectations. It seems useful to explore the factors that link ways to communicate expectations with measured achievement of course and program purposes.

Although we have not yet collected evidence, we suspect that organized academic program units are less likely than individual faculty members to have specified clear expectations for students and to have found effective ways to communicate them. Again, the view of parallel planning models suggests the notion that two different modes of communication may be needed and should be assessed separately.

Feedback. Viewing curriculum as a plan with a feedback loop fosters several levels of corrective action, each of which can stand alone or be helpful at the next organizational level. Since both expectations and assessment of student accomplishment are included in the plan, direct feedback to students is available to assist them in monitoring and planning their own educational progress. At the course level, the explicit feedback loop may help faculty members recognize and implement needed adjustments before the next course offering. Moreover, the incorporation of feedback mechanisms in most program and institutional-level plans responds to current emphasis on improving teaching and learning through assessing student outcomes.

Recognition of all types of feedback in the planning model highlights the lack of existing research to guide the use of feedback in making regular improvements in instructional planning (see Chapter Four). Individual courses are subject to frequent informal processes of evaluation and revision by faculty members. Many faculty members mention their regular but private use of student course evaluations and estimates of student achievement. However limited these informal processes may be, it is probably fair to say that many colleges lack comparable mechanisms for revising program-level plans. The program level "curricula" tend to be stable until formal periodic review or evaluation mechanisms are initiated. Poorly defined program-level plans limit ability to use program feedback in a responsive way.

Fostering Student Involvement. Cross (1986) has proposed that faculty members act simultaneously as teachers and "classroom researchers," devising new ways to check whether their students are involved in learning and achieving stated expectations. Building on this suggestion, and viewing course development as a planning process, we asked faculty members how they knew whether students were actively involved in learning. They readily, confidently, and consistently cited a few primary ways of checking student involvement in coursework.

- In classes of five or five hundred students, observe students' faces and body language and the amount of spontaneous class participation.
- Check involvement through students' performance on quizzes, tests, and assignments.
- Pose questions to the class during lectures, as well as during discussions, and assess students' responses.
- Observe attendance. Some faculty members view good attendance as a signal that student involvement is high. Conversely, they view low attendance either as a message about their teaching or as evidence of low student effort or interest.

Institutional researchers may find these methods of assessing student involvement unsophisticated. Our limited inquiry about in-class monitoring techniques suggests to us, however, that faculty members not only lack knowledge of educational research techniques but also feel their current methods of "involvement detection" are quite adequate. Thus, efforts to implement Cross's appealing suggestion should proceed cautiously. Although we do not yet have data, we suspect that methods for assessing student involvement at the program level are even less well-developed.

Opportunity 5: Core Curricula

Examining beliefs underlying academic plans constructed by typical faculty members in diverse fields can enhance knowledge of how to bridge disciplinary gaps in constructing core curricula. Following accusations of neglect (Bennett, 1984), colleges have concentrated on rebuilding core courses, particularly in the humanities. Occasionally, such new (and frequently required) experiences for students may be hastily conceived and implemented, to assert that the institution has responded to persuasive national imperatives. From our deliberations and explorations of curriculum as an academic plan, two ideas emerge (because of limited space, we will develop them more fully elsewhere). First, there is a need to develop a conceptual framework through which the many new core programs can be assessed more systematically than core curricula have been in earlier eras. We suggest tentatively that the ideas of sequencing and arranging of content (discussed earlier) may be of considerable importance (Stark and others, in progress). Second, our exploration of course planning has revealed several discipline-related assumptions and teaching strategies that must be articulated and addressed if successful cross-disciplinary courses are to endure (Stark and others, in progress).

Implications for Institutional Research

The 1990s may emerge as the golden age of opportunity for institutional researchers interested in curricular problems. Even those who have other primary interests will want to be resources on their campuses, as studies concerned with student academic development are demanded. Clearly, we are recommending that a guiding framework for this research effort is needed. We believe viewing curriculum as a plan, one specifically designed to enhance student growth and improve instruction, has great potential for guiding course and program evaluation. Beyond this general concern, we mention here some important related contributions institutional researchers could make.

1. In our research we found that, even on the same campus, dis-

cussions falter because academic terms have no consistent meaning. This is true not only for the term *curriculum* but also for such everyday terms as *academic program, developmental course, core curriculum, syllabus, expectations, feedback,* and the like. For our own purposes, we have proposed several definitions that may be useful in both two- and four-year colleges (Stark and Lowther, 1986). As institutional researchers help to carry out new types of studies in their institutions, they should actively attempt to establish and share useful definitions that will lead to consistent or compatible research and databases. We urge caution, however, in accepting existing theoretical constructs without field-testing. As an example, consider the common notion of student-centered versus subject-centered teaching. This dichotomy has been posited by theorists (Dressel and Marcus, 1982), but when we asked faculty members to characterize their departments or programs on such a continuum, they consistently told us that the dichotomy did not make sense. In faculty terms, both the student and the subject are important; one reaches the student through the subject or teaches the subject best by taking into account student needs. Consequently, this theoretical continuum was of little use as a dimension characterizing academic programs.

2. As discussed earlier, faculty members do not recognize a wide variety of service offices and resources on campuses as affecting how they plan their courses. Even on campuses where instructional development efforts exist, most faculty members we interviewed did not name any source on campus that might help them improve their instruction. When queried more directly, they indicated either lack of knowledge of such sources or a belief that the service offices could provide little help. Institutional researchers generally may wish to play a stronger role in documenting the helpfulness and success of various campus services available to improve advisement, teaching, and learning.

3. Faculty members base course planning strongly on their sense of students' characteristics, including previous preparation, anticipated effort, and (less often) concern for personal and family obligations. Yet student profile information is seldom available to faculty members prior to the first class. Consequently, experienced teachers assume, rightly or wrongly, that student characteristics are consistent from term to term. Because instructors frequently believe that obtaining student profile information is impossible, some spend time informally assessing student characteristics during the first weeks of each term. Except in open-door institutions with last-minute course registration, there seems little excuse for not enlisting campus computers and existing databases in the service of instructional improvement.

4. Discipline characteristics, program goals, and college goals that underlie faculty course and program planning vary in potency but frequently are not fully articulated. In our open-ended discussions with

faculty members, they acknowledged college and program missions as factors in course planning primarily when these issues were being actively discussed on campus. If colleges are interested in ensuring that faculty members are fully aware of distinctive missions, then continuous mission refinement and reaffirmation may be an important strategy. Working with faculty at the program level, institutional researchers can contribute much to this effort, helping to define the arena, assisting with research in the disciplinary context, and preparing interpretations for important publics.

References

Association of American Colleges. *Integrity in the College Curriculum: A Report to the Academic Community.* Washington, D.C.: Association of American Colleges, 1985.

Bennett, W. *To Reclaim a Legacy.* Washington, D.C.: National Endowment for the Humanities, 1984.

Bergquist, W. H., Gould, R., and Greenberg, E. *Designing Undergraduate Education: A Systematic Guide.* San Francisco: Jossey-Bass, 1981.

Boyer, C., and McGuinness, A., Jr., "State Initiatives to Improve Undergraduate Education: ECS Survey Highlights." *AAHE Bulletin,* 1986, *38* (6), 3-7.

Clark, C. M., and Peterson, P. L. "Teachers' Thought Processes." In M. C. Wittrock (ed.), *Handbook of Research on Teaching.* (3rd ed.) New York: Macmillan, 1986.

Confrey, J. "Conceptual Change Analysis: Implications for Mathematics and Curriculum." *Curriculum Inquiry,* 1981, *11* (3), 243-257.

Conrad, C. F., and Pratt, A. M. "Research on Academic Programs: An Inquiry into an Emerging Field." In J. Smart (ed.), *Higher Education: Handbook of Theory and Research.* Vol. 2. New York: Agathon, 1986.

Cross, K. P. "Taking Teaching Seriously." Address presented at the National Conference on Higher Education, American Association for Higher Education, Washington, D.C., 1986.

Dressel, P. L. *Improving Degree Programs: A Guide to Curriculum Development, Administration, and Review.* San Francisco: Jossey-Bass, 1980.

Dressel, P. L., and Marcus, D. *On Teaching and Learning in College: Reemphasizing the Roles of Learners and the Disciplines in Liberal Education.* San Francisco: Jossey-Bass, 1982.

Dyer, H. "Can Institutional Research Lead to a Science of Institutions?" *The Educational Record,* 1966, *47,* 452-466.

Ewell, P. *The Self-Regarding Institution: Information for Excellence.* Boulder, Colo: National Center for Higher Education Management Systems, 1984.

Gay, G. "Conceptual Models of the Curriculum Planning Process." In A. W. Foshay (ed.), *Considered Action for Curriculum Improvement.* Washington, D.C.: Association for Supervision and Curriculum Development, 1980.

King, A. R., and Brownell, J. A. *The Curriculum and the Disciplines of Knowledge: A Theory of Curriculum Practice.* New York: Wiley, 1966.

Mentkowski, M., and Doherty, A. "Abilities That Last a Lifetime." *AAHE Bulletin,* 1984, *36* (6), 3-14.

NIE Study Group on the Conditions of Excellence in American Higher Education. *Involvement in Learning: Realizing the Potential of American Higher Education.* Washington, D.C.: U.S. Government Printing Office, 1984.

Northeast Missouri State University. *In Pursuit of Degrees with Integrity: A Value-Added Approach to Undergraduate Assessment.* Washington, D.C.: American Association of State Colleges and Universities, 1984.

Office of Educational Research and Improvement. RFP Number OERI-R-86-0016. United States Contracts and Grants Management Division, Department of Education, 1986.

Pascarella, E. T. "College Environmental Influences on Learning and Cognitive Development: A Critical Review and Synthesis." In J. Smart (ed.), *Higher Education: Handbook of Theory and Research.* Vol. 1. New York: Agathon, 1985.

Phenix, P. *Realms of Meaning: A Philosophy of the Curriculum for General Education.* New York: McGraw-Hill, 1964.

Posner, G. J., and Rudnitsky, A. C. *Course Design: A Guide to Curriculum Development for Teachers.* (2nd ed.) New York: Longman, 1982.

Schwab, J. J. "The Structure of the Disciplines: Meaning and Significance." In G. W. Ford and L. Pugno (eds.), *The Structure of Knowledge and the Curriculum.* Chicago: Rand McNally, 1964.

Stark, J. S., and Lowther, M. A. *Designing the Learning Plan: A Review of Research and Theory Related to College Curricula.* Ann Arbor: National Center for Research to Improve Postsecondary Teaching and Learning, University of Michigan, 1986.

Stark, J. S., Lowther, M. A., Ryan, M. P., Bomotti, S. S., Genthon, M., Haven, C. L., and Martens, G. *Faculty and Students Talk About Course Design: A Technical Report.* Ann Arbor: National Center for Research to Improve Postsecondary Teaching and Learning, University of Michigan, in progress.

Taba, H. *Curriculum Development: Theory and Practice.* New York: Harcourt Brace Jovanovich, 1962.

Toombs, W. "The Application of Design-Based Curriculum Analysis to General Education." *Higher Education Review,* 1977–78, *1,* 18–29.

Winter, D. G., McClelland, D. C., and Stewart, A. J. *A New Case for the Liberal Arts: Assessing Institutional Goals and Student Development.* San Francisco: Jossey-Bass, 1982.

Joan S. Stark is professor of higher education, researcher in the Center for the Study of Higher and Postsecondary Education, and director of the National Center for Research to Improve Postsecondary Teaching and Learning (NCRIPTAL), at the University of Michigan.

Malcolm A. Lowther is professor of education, research faculty member in the Center for the Study of Higher and Postsecondary Education, and a senior researcher in the National Center for Research to Improve Postsecondary Teaching and Learning (NCRIPTAL), at the University of Michigan.

Traditional ideas about improving teaching, which focus on reward systems and teacher preparation, should be augmented by new understandings of faculty self-perception and motivation.

Faculty Motivation and Teaching

Janet H. Lawrence

How does one predict and influence faculty behavior? Management models of behavioral change, borrowed from the business sector, do not transfer readily to postsecondary institutions. The lack of fit is due, in part, to differences in organizational goals and structures. However, for institutional researchers and college administrators, our lack of knowledge about the motivational processes that affect faculty role performance compounds the problem of influencing change.

Higher education researchers have looked primarily to changing the organization of postsecondary institutions (for example, departmental arrangements, tenure, and promotion policies), believing that differences in their social structures and processes account, in large part, for faculty motivation problems. A key question for these investigators has been how the structure of the faculty role and career socialization experiences contribute to variations in professional behavior (see, for example, Light, 1974; Parsons and Platt, 1968).

Some years ago, the primary interest of researchers was in differences across academic settings that might affect motivation (Wilson, 1941;

The author gratefully acknowledges the contributions of Virginia Polk Okoloko to the writing of this chapter.

Lazarsfeld and Thielens, 1958), but in the 1960s and 1970s the focus was broadened to include differences among the disciplines as well (Light, 1974; Parsons and Platt, 1968). During the 1970s, with growing interest in adult development and concern about the aging professoriate, a new emphasis appeared in the literature. Researchers began to consider how individual differences in psychological need states and perceptions might affect faculty behavior at a given time and over time (Baldwin, 1979; Bayer and Dutton, 1977; Kanter, 1977; Lawrence and Blackburn, 1985).

Many suggestions for changing or maintaining faculty effort in teaching have accompanied the research. These suggestions range from highly individualized counseling programs to recommendations for sweeping professional reforms. However, two general types of solutions to enhancing faculty motivation have predominated: reward and preparation. In this chapter, several key assumptions of reward and preparation are critiqued, and the discussion is used to explain why these solutions are difficult to implement and thus meet with mixed success. The need for research in the cognitive aspects of motivation is elaborated. The goal is to stimulate among institutional researchers some new thinking about a persistent issue.

Reward solutions require changes in the organization that will induce faculty members to improve their teaching. In these solutions, the key to changing faculty behavior is the environment. It is assumed that if administrators create a climate or context that encourages good teaching (by rewarding good performance, providing resources, or offering other inducements to improve), professors will respond. They could do better if only they were rightfully encouraged.

Preparation solutions, in contrast, press for changes in the education of professors as teachers, or for greater emphasis on demonstrated teaching skill at the time of hiring. Advocates of improved preparation believe a lack of knowledge about the teaching-learning process is the primary cause of inadequate instruction. Although at some point these distinctions break down (for example, the optimal solution may involve both rewards and preparation), these general types of solutions are useful in focusing attention on the inadequacy of currently reported research and in highlighting avenues institutional researchers might follow.

Both reward and preparation solutions assume that the social context of postsecondary institutions influences faculty values and behaviors. Both also make some key, but different, assumptions about professors' expertise in and motivation for teaching, as well as about the impact of evaluation on role performance.

Very little attention has been given to how professors process information about their institutions and about their role performance, or to how these perceptions affect work-related decisions. Self-competence (a person's subjective rating of his ability to perform certain acts) and self-efficacy (a person's expectation that her actions will lead to desired outcomes) are theoretical constructs that may help explain why professors in the same organizational context invest different amounts of time in teaching, and why they vary in their responses to performance feedback and institutional incentives. In the last section of this chapter, I describe an alternative research paradigm that incorporates professors' beliefs about their ability to do what is expected of them (self-competence) and about their influence over institutional decisions and student learning (self-efficacy). Practical questions are raised within this framework.

Changing Academic Culture

Reward solutions depend on a set of core institutional values and beliefs, as well as on social structures and processes that encourage faculty conformity. From this perspective, environment determines behavior. Preparation solutions also assume that environment has some influence on behavior, but the success of preparation recommendations does not depend on altering the culture. The goal of reward solutions is to manipulate the social context, but the goal of preparation solutions is to improve individual teaching directly.

Do institutional values and reinforcement mechanisms exist? To be sure, there are studies that point to campus differences in terms of faculty values and preferred role activities. After reviewing the extensive literature on this topic, Finkelstein (1984) concluded that variations in general role performance of faculty members can be represented as differences between research universities and elite liberal arts colleges, on the one hand, and all other institutions, on the other. Faculty members in these two types of institutions differ in (1) their preferences for research, teaching, and service; (2) the effort they give to these facets of the faculty role; and (3) the nature of their identification with the institutions. With respect to teaching specifically, institutional type appeared to be a better predictor of instructional practice than were individual faculty goals (Gaff and Wilson, 1975).

The literature suggests that the variations across campuses are primarily the result of hiring practices, faculty role structures, and reward systems. In short, faculty selection processes can result in the hiring of individuals who share and maintain the values of the institution, the status quo (Blau, 1974). Fluctuations in workload and effort can be attributed to institutional norms for course loads and research (Finkelstein, 1984). Correlations between salary level and distribution of effort have led other researchers to conclude that rewards result in faculty conformity with the predominant expectations (Tuckman, 1976).

Studies also suggest that selective reinforcement of behavior during career socialization experiences may contribute to institutional differences in professors' behavior and values. For example, in a research university Lawrence and Blackburn (1985) found that publication rates tended to peak around times of tenure and promotion. Further evidence of the impact of socialization is provided by Clark, Corcoran, and Lewis (1984), who found that professors were aware of their universities' norms about the timing of certain career events and accomplishments. Faculty knew if their career progress was slower or faster than that of their colleagues.

In contrast with the body of literature that portrays a college faculty working in concert toward institutional goals, there are studies that suggest great diversity in priorities. Turning first to the question of shared values, Blank (1976) uncovered intrainstitutional discrepancies between the goals individual professors held for their teaching and the goals institutions held for their students. Other researchers have found systematic variations across faculty subgroups in terms of their values and behavior. For instance, professors on the same campus who differ in their disciplinary backgrounds or career stages are likely to have different role expectations for faculty (Zuckerman, 1973; Baldwin, 1979; Lawrence, 1984; Bayer and Dutton, 1977) and for students (Gaff and Wilson, 1975; Stark and Morstain, 1978). In addition, professors who did their graduate work in highly ranked institutions are likely to have different career goals and values from those of colleagues who graduated from universities held in lower regard (Blackburn, Brehymer, and Hall, 1978).

Does this diversity in values and beliefs diminish as institutional sanctions are brought to bear on a faculty group? Borland (1970) found faculty members were quite autonomous in the allocation of effort to different activities. In contrast with Tuckman (1976), Borland's general conclusion was that professors' goals and behaviors can be impervious to institutional rewards. This conclusion has been supported by other researchers, who have found that although teaching is not financially rewarded to the same extent as publication, faculty do work to improve in this area (Kasten, 1984; Siegfried and White, 1973; O'Connell, 1983). As these examples illustrate, evidence of the relation between salary incentives and role performance is mixed. It is unfortunate, therefore, that researchers have not used quasi-experimental designs that would enable them to identify antecedents to behavioral change in colleges with and without merit salary programs.

Incentives other than salary have, of course, been used in attempts to modify faculty teaching behavior. These include grants, awards, release time to work on teaching projects, and provision of media and instructional design support services. Data regarding faculty perceptions of the effectiveness of these arrangements have been gathered (Centra, 1976). Unfortunately, however, there are few published studies on the extent to which these incentives affect professors' actual teaching practice or enhance student learning (Meeker, 1977).

At the National Center for Research to Improve Postsecondary Teaching and Learning (NCRIPTAL), we have interviewed professors in diverse settings (a traditionally black institution, rural and urban community colleges, liberal arts colleges, and comprehensive universities). The interviews cover a range of topics, including institutional decision making, characteristics of professors valued on their campuses, attribution of responsibility for different decisions, and self-competence assessments. One of the goals has been to determine if faculty hold beliefs about an institution (its goals, priorities, expectations for students) that influence their behavior. Our preliminary analyses of these interview data confirm Bayer's (1973) finding that professors tend to have a common understanding of institutional priorities and to share very general goals for their students. However, the data also reveal that faculty members do not necessarily agree on what they should do as teachers to facilitate student achievement of mutually agreeable objectives.

To illustrate, although two community college professors were equally aware of the school's general goal to prepare students for college-level study, they exhibited different behaviors. One of them cancelled class when students had not done the assigned readings. The rationale for this behavior was that students "need to learn to work independently and to be responsible." The other professor reorganized class time so that more assignments were done during supervised study halls. These individuals reported different levels of informal collegial support, as well as formal sanctions on their conduct. However, it was clear that when they are convinced that what they are doing is right for students, these professors will persist in their current teaching behavior.

This vignette illustrates the complex interplay that may occur between the formal and informal aspects of a college environment and the individual perceptions of a situation. Professors' beliefs about what they ought to be doing are sometimes more predictive of actual role performance than the institution's expectations and rewards. Consequently, neither administrators nor faculty members should take for granted the premises that underlie recommendations for changing faculty behavior when these involve modifications in role structures or selective reinforcement. Institutional researchers would be well advised to examine the fit between faculty perceptions and the rationale for changes being proposed by administrators.

Enhancing Faculty Expertise

Preparation solutions take the position that inappropriate teaching stems primarily from a lack of knowledge about the teaching-learning process. This orientation differs from that underlying reward solutions, which may assume either that faculty members lack knowledge about the teaching-learning process or that they have the expertise but, because of environmental constraints, do not fully use their knowledge. Both reward and preparation solutions imply there is a best method of teaching. However, in the case of the preparation solutions, there also is an assumption that the current preparation of faculty as teachers is inadequate.

Research comparing the relative effectiveness of teaching methods is extensive and points to some broad generalizations about practice. When the overall course objective is acquisition of information, lectures, compared to other methods, may not lead to significantly different student achievement. In contrast, class discussions seem to be better than lectures when the goals are to change attitudes or to develop problem-solving skills (Kulik and Kulik, 1979; Levenson-Rose and Menges, 1981). The picture becomes more complex when other outcome criteria, such as the durability of learning, are taken into account (Cohen, Ebeling, and Kulik, 1981). By and large, the reviewers of teaching-method research have concluded that the results are far from consistent and certainly do not underscore the superiority of any one instructional technique.

Educational commentators assert that the lack of systematic attention to the preparation of graduate students as teachers of their disciplines leads to the perpetuation of poor teaching because graduate students ultimately model their own teaching after that of their professors. However, there is little or no research that examines the relationship between graduate teaching preparation and effectiveness as a college instructor.

The NCRIPTAL interviews suggest that professors believe they are competent teachers of their subject matter. Most will admit, though, that they feel ill prepared to teach students who are not ready for college-level study. In some instances this may be blaming the victim, but, generally speaking, the respondents appear to be sincere in their answers. In schools with less selective or open admissions, the student diversity is great. How does one cope with the range of ability in a class?

Diagnosing and finding solutions for the problem are complex tasks that may go well beyond what professors are prepared to do. Institutions may not provide the instructional design expertise and the support services that are needed in these situations. Furthermore, successful interventions probably require a collective effort of several professors as much as individual change.

In sum, the effectiveness of teaching practices must be evaluated in relation to goals. While professors may not be well versed in instructional methods, it does not necessarily follow that they are ineffective teachers. Controversy will probably always surround the question of whether the instructor's teaching method (Grasha, 1977) or his or her personal characteristics contribute most to students' learning (Bruton and Crull, 1982).

The Influences on Teaching Motivation

Advocates of preparation solutions generally believe that faculty members are motivated by the teaching act itself, whereas proponents of reward solutions take the stance that this intrinsic incentive is weak. The research on faculty motivation tends to rely heavily on behavioristic and need or drive paradigms, in which the impetus to act is assumed to derive from conditions set by administrators or from age-related or career-stage needs (Staw, 1983). Hence, there is only indirect evidence about whether or not professors devote effort to teaching because the activity itself is appealing.

As noted earlier, several researchers have found that professors in universities where research productivity is highly rewarded still initiate and sustain efforts to improve their teaching. They do it, McKeachie (1979) and others argue, because they find teaching to be personally gratifying.

Some writers take the opposite position. They argue that doctoral study leads to strong research values, which enhance the intrinsic appeal of scholarship and diminish the motivation to teach (Ladd, 1979). Still others believe the effort devoted to teaching varies by career age, and that older professors are more interested in and give more time to this activity as a result of developmental needs (Baldwin, 1979).

This brief review illustrates how inconclusive our knowledge is about why faculty activities vary. The literature is further constrained because the frame of reference in most studies has been the individual professor working on her or his class (that is, a focus on the motivation for individual achievement), rather than on collective faculty efforts toward institutional reform. Although the attraction of classroom instruction is qualitatively different from the appeal of the group task, this important distinction typically has not been acknowledged in commentaries about faculty motivation. One must be careful about generalizing across these situations. It may well be that organizational incentives are required to stimulate faculty effort toward making major programmatic changes. Such incentives may be less critical when the goal is to motivate professors to enhance student learning in the courses they have themselves developed.

The Role of Evaluation

The success of both reward and preparation solutions may hinge on administrators' ability to create a system of evaluation (for example, performance assessment) that induces professors to change their behavior. In reward situations, a common task is to establish the relative standing of professors for the purpose of merit salary allocation or other extrinsic awards. When the objective is to enhance teachers' expertise, the goal is to provide diagnostic feedback on the strengths and weaknesses of their teaching. However, in both cases, the timing and the nature of the evaluation are critical.

Writing about behavioral modification theories and the implications of different reinforcement schedules for managing faculty behavior, Staw (1983) concluded that higher educators must guard against overrewarding teaching, research, or service. He cites psychological research showing that people's attraction to an activity itself can diminish if they come to believe they do it for the reward. However, Staw's review reveals that research on the impact of alternative faculty reinforcement plans is lacking.

The timing of feedback resulting from assessment of teaching performance is a question that has received systematic attention (McKeachie and Kulik, 1975). On balance, the data suggest that student evaluations of teaching typically are not done at the optimal time for provoking changes in classroom instruction. Faculty members seem to be more responsive to assessment that occurs midcourse than to evaluations done (as is usually the case) at the end of the term.

While factor-analytic studies of student evaluations have provided general indices of the dimensions of effective teaching (McKeachie and Kulik, 1975), we know little about the nature of feedback that would lead ineffective teachers to change. It is reasonable to assume that evaluation viewed as credible is more likely to be compelling.

If credibility is a critical property of feedback, it is difficult to accept that professors will change in response to student evaluations. For one thing, faculty self-evaluations do not mirror students' or colleagues' ratings of them as teachers (Blackburn and Clark, 1975). Furthermore, when Benton (1982) reviewed a large share of the criterion-validity studies, he found only modest correlations between student evaluations and student achievement. As Cohen (1981) points out, it may be unrealistic to expect more than moderate correlations, because of individual differences in student characteristics. Nevertheless, McKeachie and Kulik (1975) conclude that "perhaps the most impressive thing about studies relating class achievement to class ratings of instructors is the inconsistency of the results" (p. 235).

Professors in our NCRIPTAL interviews were quite critical of summative teaching ratings used in merit salary decisions. In different ways, they said that numerical indices trivialized the teaching activity. Feedback from classroom visits by department chairs or faculty designees also was discounted if the respondent thought the person was unable to place observations in the context of the entire course. It seems unlikely that linking such forms of teaching evaluation to salary incentives will lead to changes in professional behavior. The likelihood is further diminished by the dollar amount of salary increases involved. Many respondents said that potential salary increases for raising scores on student ratings were insufficient to encourage change; personal motivation was essential.

The comments of instructors we interviewed suggested that the successful use of student evaluations as diagnostic feedback depends on professors' perceptions of links between their current activities and their long-term objectives for learners. Faculty members dismissed certain criticisms of their teaching when they believed their classroom activities would benefit students eventually. An English literature professor who was criticized for disorganization, for example, simply smiled; she wanted to create an environment that provoked students into formulating their own integrative frameworks. A chemistry professor who was told that the weekly quizzes in his introductory course were excessive ignored the student criticism, because his colleagues had said that his students did well in advanced courses. In one respondent's words, professors are "ready to sacrifice current popularity for long-term impact." Unfortunately, there are few studies that determine whether faculty members selectively rationalize persisting in behavior that students consistently rate low.

Do professors change in response to longitudinal data? A few institutions (for example, the University of Washington and the University of Wisconsin) have gathered data from graduates that could provide professors with feedback judgments about their instruction over the long term. However, information about faculty response to this kind of assessment has not appeared in the higher education literature.

In sum, existing research does not provide consistent support for the key assumptions of either the reward or the preparation solutions. Furthermore, there is very little empirical evidence on the effectiveness of the different institutional practices of either type. Together, these conditions underscore the need to gather more systematic data regarding the core assumptions of these practices and to examine the question of faculty motivation from different theoretical perspectives.

The Importance of Faculty Self-Perceptions

In most cases, faculty members enjoy great autonomy in deciding how they will carry out their general responsibilities—teaching, research, and service. Admittedly, the environment places certain constraints on what they can do (for example, because the service contract on the computers has not been renewed, a professor cannot count on using them in class); but a professor's perceptions of this environment and subjective evaluations of his or her capacity to work under these conditions are also important.

Considering the arguments for and against the various proposals for changing teaching behavior, it is clear that researchers have been remiss in not giving more attention to how professors view their own behavior. The chances of inducing faculty members to devote more effort to teaching their own classes, as well as to cooperative curricular projects, are enhanced if one understands how professors make decisions about their activities. Therefore, our research on faculty is focusing on the cognitive aspects of motivation—how professors' perceptions of their institutions affect their role performance.

The psychological literature on motivation, especially the portion written by social and cognitive psychologists, has been used to frame the NCRIPTAL research agenda for our program *Faculty as a Key Resource.* In particular, self-competence and self-efficacy (Bandura, 1977) have been identified as important theoretical constructs to explore, because they take into account people's beliefs about their capacity to do what is expected, as well as their perceptions that what they do (teaching, research, or service) is of any consequence (for example, the idea that working on major curricular changes will actually lead to reform and desired student outcomes). It seems reasonable to expect that, given choices, professors will devote time to activities they believe they do well and that are likely to have an impact on their fields and on students.

Some important research questions emerge. Are faculty members who believe they are competent teachers less likely to change in response to evaluation by students? Do they find that some types of feedback are more persuasive than others? Is the professor who believes faculty efforts have little effect on academic decisions more or less willing to work on general curricular reforms like critical thinking or writing across the curriculum? Is such an individual's participation contingent on first changing her or his perceptions of the decision-making process?

Rather than make a priori decisions about the characteristics of valued professors, my colleagues and I have been experimenting with a research technique used by Sternberg and others (1981). We have been asking professors to describe the attributes of a prototype of a valued faculty member on their campuses, to explain why they chose these particular attributes, and to evaluate themselves in relation to each attribute. In this way, we get a sense of the characteristics that comprise the prototype and the extent to which these characteristics are the result of environmental factors (for example, the idea that only productive scholars are given tenure). We also gain a sense of the individual personality differences or abilities that people bring to the teaching role, and we obtain self-competence assessments in relation to a meaningful abstraction—the valued professor on the respondent's campus.

As we move through our research agenda, we believe we will develop new insights into faculty motivation. Higher educators have known for a long time that students' perceptions of a learning environment affect their motivation levels. It is time to assess the impact of these cognitive processes on faculty, who play a key role in establishing the teaching-learning environment.

References

Baldwin, R. "Adult and Career Development: What Are the Implications for Faculty?" *Current Issues in Higher Education,* 1979, *2,* 13-20.

Bandura, A. "Self-Efficacy: Toward A Unifying Theory of Behavioral Change." *Psychological Review,* 1977, *84,* 191-215.

Bayer, A. E. *Teaching Faculty in Academe: 1972-1973.* American Council on Education Research Reports. Vol. 8, no. 2. Washington, D.C.: American Council on Education, 1973.

Bayer, A. E., and Dutton, J. E. "Career Age and Research-Professional Activities of Academic Scientists." *Journal of Higher Education,* 1977, *48,* 259-282.

Benton, S. *Rating College Teaching: Criterion Validity Studies of Student Evaluation-of-Instruction Instruments.* AAHE-ERIC/Higher Education Research Report no. 1. Washington, D.C.: American Association for Higher Education, 1982.

Blackburn, R. T., Brehymer, C. E., and Hall, D. E. "Correlates of Faculty Publications." *Sociology of Education,* 1978, *51,* 132-141.

Blackburn, R. T., and Clark, M. J. "An Assessment of Faculty Performance: Some Correlates Between Administrator, Colleague, Student, and Self-Ratings." *Sociology of Education,* 1975, *48,* 242-256.

Blank, R. K. "An Organizational Model of Academic Institutions and the Teaching Goals of Faculty Members." Unpublished doctoral dissertation, Florida State University, 1976.

Blau, P. M. *The Organization of Academic Work.* New York: Wiley, 1974.

Borland, D. "The University as an Organization: An Analysis of the Faculty Rewards System." Unpublished Ed.D. dissertation, Indiana University, 1970.

Bruton, B., and Crull, S. "Causes and Consequences of Student Evaluation of Instruction." *Research in Higher Education,* 1982, *17,* 195-206.

Centra, J. *Faculty Development Practices in U.S. Colleges and Universities.* Project Report 76-3. Princeton, N.J.: Educational Testing Service, 1976.

Clark, S., Corcoran, M., and Lewis, D. R. "Critical Perspectives on Faculty Career Development, with Implications for Differential Institutional Policies." Paper presented at the annual meeting of the American Educational Research Association, New Orleans, April 1984.

Cohen, P. "Student Ratings of Instruction and Student Achievement: A Meta-Analysis of Multisection Validity Studies." *Review of Educational Research,* 1981, *51,* 281-309.

Cohen, P., Ebeling, B., and Kulik, J. "A Meta-Analysis of Outcome Studies of Visual-Based Instruction." *Educational Communication and Technology,* 1981, *29,* 26-36.

Finkelstein, M. J. *The American Academic Profession: A Synthesis of Social Scientific Inquiry Since World War II.* Columbus: Ohio State University Press, 1984.

Gaff, J. G., and Wilson, R. C. "Faculty Impact on Students." In R. C. Wilson and others (eds.), *College Professors and Their Impact on Students.* New York: Wiley, 1975.

Grasha, A. *Assessing and Developing Faculty Performance: Principles and Models.* Cincinnati, Ohio: Communication and Education Associates, 1977.

Kanter, R. M. *Men and Women of the Organization.* New York: Basic Books, 1977.

Kasten, K. "Tenure and Merit Pay as Rewards for Research, Teaching, and Service at a Research University." *Journal of Higher Education,* 1984, *55,* 500-514.

Kulik, J., and Kulik, C. "College Teaching." In P. Peterson and H. Walberg (eds.), *Research on Teaching*. Berkeley, Calif.: McCutcheon, 1979.

Ladd, E. C. "The Work Experience of American College Professors: Some Data and an Argument." *Current Issues in Higher Education—1979*. Washington, D.C.: American Association for Higher Education, 1979.

Lawrence, J. H. "Faculty Age and Teaching." In C.M.N. Mehrotra (ed.), *Teaching and Aging*. New Directions for Teaching and Learning, no. 19. San Francisco: Jossey-Bass, 1984.

Lawrence, J. H., and Blackburn, R. T. "Faculty Careers: Maturation, Demographic, and Historical Effects." *Research in Higher Education*, 1985, *22* (2), 17, 19, 20, 26.

Lazarsfeld, P. F., and Thielens, W., Jr. *The Academic Mind: Social Scientists in a Time of Crisis*. Glencoe, Ill.: The Free Press, 1958.

Levenson-Rose, J., and Menges, R. "Improving College Teaching: A Critical Review of Research." *Review of Educational Research*, 1981, *51*, 403–434.

Light, D. W., Jr. "Introduction: The Structure of the Academic Professions." *Sociology of Education*, 1974, *47* (1), 18.

McKeachie, W. J. "Perspectives from Psychology: Financial Incentives Are Ineffective for Faculty." In D. R. Lewis and W. E. Becker, Jr. (eds.), *Academic Rewards in Higher Education*. Cambridge, Mass.: Ballinger, 1979.

McKeachie, W. J., and Kulik, J. "Effective College Teaching." In F. Kerlinger (ed.), *Review of Research in Teaching*. Vol. 3. Itasca, Ill.: Peacock Press, 1975.

Meeker, J. "An Evaluation of Faculty Support Programs at Three Research Universities." Unpublished Ph.D. dissertation, University of Michigan, 1977.

O'Connell, C. "College Policies Off-Target in Fostering Faculty Development." *Journal of Higher Education*, 1983, *54* (6), 662–675.

Parsons, T., and Platt, G. M. "The American Academic Profession: A Pilot Study." National Science Foundation Grant GS 513, 1968.

Siegfried, J. J., and White, K. J. "Teaching and Publishing as Determinants of Academic Salaries." *Journal of Economic Education*, 1973, *4*, 90–98.

Stark, J. S., and Morstain, B. R. "Educational Orientations of Faculty in Liberal Arts Colleges: An Analysis of Disciplinary Differences." *Journal of Higher Education*, 1978, *49*, 420–437.

Staw, B. "Motivation Research Is the Art of Faculty Management." *Review of Higher Education*, 1983, *6*, 301–321.

Sternberg, R., Conway, B., Ketron, J., and Bernstein, M. "People's Conception of Intelligence." *Journal of Personality and Social Psychology*, 1981, *41*, 82.

Tuckman, H. P. *Publication, Teaching, and the Academic Reward Structure*. Lexington, Mass.: Heath, 1976.

Wilson, L. *The Academic Man*. London: Oxford University Press, 1941.

Zuckerman, H. "Aging and Age Structure in Science." In R. K. Merton (ed.), *The Sociology of Science: Theoretical and Empirical Investigations*. Chicago: University of Chicago Press, 1973.

Janet H. Lawrence is an associate professor in the Program in Higher and Adult Continuing Education and the Center for the Study of Higher and Postsecondary Education, a research associate in the National Center for Research to Improve Postsecondary Teaching and Learning (NCRIPTAL), and associate research scientist in the Center for Research on Learning and Teaching, at the University of Michigan.

Assessment programs designed to improve instruction should be based on strong theoretical models of student learning, motivation, and instruction.

A Process-Oriented View of Student Motivation and Cognition

Paul R. Pintrich

The current interest in postsecondary educational reform has resulted in a number of proposals focused on the improvement of college teaching and learning (Bok, 1986; Boyer, 1987; NIE Study Group, 1984). Although these calls for improvement have recommended a variety of remedies, most have suggested that assessment of teaching and learning can play an important role in improving college instruction. However, if assessment programs are to be relevant to instructional improvement efforts, they must be closely tied to instructional concerns and be based on strong theoretical models of the teaching and learning process (Haney, 1984; Linn, 1986; Sternberg, 1985).

Accordingly, this chapter presents a general theoretical approach to college student learning that should be useful to institutional researchers as they help to design assessment programs relevant to instructional improvement efforts. The general approach is based on current cognitive and information-processing models of student motivation and cognition, which provide a functional description of the psychology of the learner that is readily applicable to problems in the psychology of instruction.

J. S. Stark and L. A. Mets (eds.). *Improving Teaching and Learning Through Research.*
New Directions for Institutional Research, no. 57. San Francisco: Jossey-Bass, Spring 1988.

The Information-Processing Approach to Student Motivation and Cognition

Paralleling recent work in cognitive and instructional psychology (Pintrich and others, 1986), an information-processing approach offers a promising framework to discuss assessment, teaching, and learning in postsecondary settings and provides a common language for a wide range of educational phenomena. Not only are most experimental, social, developmental, instructional, and differential psychologists now using the same paradigm, but so are researchers on educational media and technology, instructional design, and classroom teaching. The confluence of all these different types of researchers who find information processing theory a useful theoretical framework for addressing psychological questions provides a rich store of knowledge to draw on in discussing teaching and learning.

Information-processing views of development assume that student progress can best be characterized by quantitative, not qualitative, change in students' thinking or behavior. Many information-processing models have attempted to sort people into different subgroups, on the basis of knowledge base (for example, the research on experts and novices, like Chi, 1978) or use of strategies (for example, the research on learning strategies and metacognition, like Weinstein and Mayer, 1986). The following sections discuss four aspects of student learning that are relevant to teaching and learning in postsecondary settings: student knowledge, learning strategies, critical thinking and problem solving, and motivation.

Students' Knowledge. Many current information-processing models of learning stress the importance of the nature and organization of the student's knowledge base for performance. For example, studies of experts' versus novices' memory for chess positions or dinosaurs' names have demonstrated the importance of knowledge for performance (Chi, 1978). In addition, studies of school-related areas like reading, mathematics, physics, computer programming, and social science have all shown that effective problem solving in these domains depends on students' knowledge in that domain (Bransford, Sherwood, Vye, and Rieser, 1986). These information-processing views of student knowledge stress the organization of the students' knowledge into cognitive structures, schemata, cognitive representations, production systems, or propositional networks, to name a few of the labels used to describe the organization of student knowledge (McKeachie, Pintrich, Lin, and Smith, 1986).

Although there are important theoretical differences among these labels, a few commonalities are relevant for assessment issues. These knowledge structures are assumed to be internal, cognitive representations of the subject area. The students' structures are based on the content and structure of the information presented in class, but students actively create their own structures in the process of learning and integrating new course information with prior knowledge. These cognitive structures help students store and organize new information, thereby guiding future perceptions and learning. Although these cognitive structures are internal, cognitive representations, they can be inferred and described by objective measures (McKeachie, Pintrich, Lin, and Smith, 1986) and represent the "students' public understanding of a discipline" (Shavelson, 1983).

How is this information-processing, cognitive-structure view of student knowledge relevant to college teaching and learning? It is likely that college students learn a great deal of content knowledge in different courses, and that students' level of content knowledge is assessed rather well by class tests and final examinations. However, the relevance of the information-processing approach lies in the assumption that it is not just the amount or quantity of knowledge that a student possesses, but also the qualitative organization and structure of that knowledge that is important for future performance. As McKeachie and others (1986) point out, if an important goal of higher education is to foster lifelong learning, then the student must be able to use the knowledge gained in a course after the final examination. This is not likely to happen if the information is just a compilation or accumulation of unrelated facts, principles, and theories. The information must be organized and elaborated in a meaningful fashion. The difficult and important issues of how students acquire meaningful knowledge and how instruction can facilitate that process are beyond the scope of this chapter, but the assessment of student knowledge and how that assessment information may be used to improve teaching and learning are relevant issues.

A variety of methods have been used in attempts to measure students' cognitive or knowledge structures (see McKeachie and others, 1986). There are two general approaches: a direct method, and an indirect method.

In the variations of the direct method, students are asked to arrange key concepts or propositions from the course in some structured, spatial manner to reflect understanding of the course material (for example, by drawing maps, networks, or other pictorial, graphic representations of the relationships among the concepts). The resulting product is scored according to preset criteria and used as a measure of a student's cognitive structure.

In contrast, the indirect methods do not ask students to produce actual spatial representation of the relationships among the concepts. Rather, indirect methods include word association, sorting, and ordered-tree or interview techniques that are used to infer cognitive structures from how students sort or arrange lists of concepts.

These techniques can be used to examine the development of students' cognitive structures during a term. Research has demonstrated that students progress toward more organized and hierarchical structures over a semester course. Students' cognitive structures have been shown to be correlated with their achievement in class, but not to such an extent that achievement and structure have seemed to be measuring the same construct. In addition, students' structures have been shown to become more elaborated and more similar to instructors' cognitive structures over a semester (Naveh-Benjamin, McKeachie, Lin, and Tucker, 1986).

This type of measure has a number of applications for assessment, as well as for teaching and learning. It can be used by institutional researchers or instructors to assess students' cognitive structures for course material. It provides a measure of student performance in a course that is related to achievement on examinations, but it reflects students' organization, not just their recall of material. This information can be used by instructors to assess their own teaching and manner of organizing course content. In addition, the method can be used as a teaching tool in the classroom to improve student learning. The construction of cognitive structures by students, and the explicit comparison of student structures with faculty structures, facilitate discussion of course content. For example, the discussion of different models for understanding and organizing the course material seems to help students comprehend some of the underlying relationships among the course concepts. In addition, it assists students in seeing that there are different ways of accurately representing course materials (there is no one "right" answer). This method can also help faculty members improve their teaching, because it makes their goals and preferred structures for the organization of course material explicit. For example, in discussions of cognitive structure with faculty members from several disciplines (English composition and literature, biology, ecology, sociology), the method has provided a means for clarifying the goals of a course and the instructional strategies for achieving them. Faculty members can then decide if they want to adjust their instructional goals and strategies to make them more consonant with each other.

Although the content and structure of students' knowledge obviously plays an important role in their learning, it may not be sufficient for all learning situations and effective problem solving (Pintrich, Cross, Kozma, and McKeachie, 1986). Educators at all levels have become increasingly concerned about generalizable cognitive skills, such as those for processing information, thinking critically, and solving problems. We shall now consider these kinds of cognitive skills.

Students' Learning Strategies. As Weinstein and Mayer (1986) point out, recent research on teaching and learning has focused on the active role of the learner in student achievement. Obviously, the subject-matter content students know when taking on a new task will influence their performance. While theories about prior knowledge and cognitive structures also are important components of a theory of learning, research on student learning strategies that deals with how the student acquires and modifies his or her knowledge base will be discussed here.

In their review of the learning-strategies literature, Weinstein and Mayer (1986) suggest that learning strategies influence the way students process information as they acquire new knowledge and modify old or prior knowledge. They suggest that four components of information processing are affected by learning strategies: selection, acquisition, construction, and integration. Other models of this process (Corno and Mandinach, 1983; Sternberg, 1985) use somewhat different terms, but the general concern is how students acquire and integrate new information with old information.

The selection process involves how attention is controlled to select certain stimuli or information from the environment and transfer those stimuli or that information to working memory. The acquisition process concerns the transfer of information from working memory to long-term memory for permanent storage. This process involves how the information is encoded by the student. In the construction process, the student actively builds connections among ideas and concepts in working memory. This construction involves building schemata and other organizational frameworks for the information, as discussed earlier. The last of these four components, integration, involves connecting new knowledge with prior knowledge, so that retrieval is facilitated in the future (McKeachie, Pintrich, Lin, and Smith, 1986). This brief description of these four components of information processing does not do justice to the complicated question of how students actually process information, but it does provide a context for the discussion of learning strategies.

Weinstein and Mayer (1986) define *learning strategy* as any thought or behavior in which a learner engages. This definition includes basic memory processes, as well as general problem-solving skills, and encompasses almost all the researched cognitive processes. In contrast, Tobias (1982) has distinguished between micro-level strategies and macro-level strategies. For Tobias, the micro-level strategies concern the basic cognitive processes (such as attention and encoding of all information), while the macro-level strategies (such as reviewing, note taking, and comprehension monitoring) concern the processing of instructional input. This distinction parallels Sternberg's (1985) distinction between performance components and metacomponents.

In terms of teaching and learning, the global level of analysis provided by a focus on macro-level strategies is more relevant (McKeachie, Pintrich, Lin, and Smith, 1986). This choice is made on theoretical, methodological, and practical grounds. A number of researchers (for example, Paris, Lipson, and Wixson, 1983) have limited their definitions of learning strategies to cognitive processes that are intentional and under control of the learner. Nevertheless, some of the basic attentional and memory processes are not really under the control of the learner; they are part of every individual's basic information-processing equipment and are elicited automatically by various tasks (see Sternberg, 1985).

Moreover, the basic cognitive microprocesses are difficult to measure unless experimental designs with carefully specified tasks are combined with the collection of reaction-time data. This is clearly not a practical option for most institutional researchers, who are concerned with assessment of teaching and learning in college settings. In addition, it is not clear that some of the experimental tasks used by cognitive psychologists in the laboratory have much ecological validity when applied to the classroom setting. Accordingly, in attempting to assess student learning strategies, institutional researchers may have to rely on other methods (for example, self-report measures) that may decrease construct validity but increase external validity (Cook and Campbell, 1979).

A variety of taxonomies are available for describing and classifying students' learning strategies (Dansereau, 1985; Pressley, 1986; Weinstein and Mayer, 1986). McKeachie and others (1986) have recently suggested a taxonomy that groups learning strategies into the three general categories of cognitive, metacognitive, and resource-management strategies (see Table 1), with several types of strategies included in each category. Basically, the cognitive strategies are assumed to help students encode new material and facilitate the organization and retrieval of information. The metacognitive strategies assist students in planning, regulating, monitoring, and modifying their cognitive processes. The resource-management strategies help students control the available resources (time, effort, outside help) for performing various academic tasks.

There have been a number of attempts to develop measures of study skills and learning strategies (Brown, 1964; Brown and Holtzman, 1967; Carter, 1958; Christensen, 1968; Goldman and Warren, 1973). However, Weinstein and Underwood (1985) have pointed out several problems with these instruments. One of the most important is that many of the instruments have no underlying theoretical frameworks. Items are included that concern such traditional areas of study skills as note taking, time management, work habits, and attitudes, but there are few items on how students actually learn or process material. In contrast, more recent approaches, like *LASSI (The Learning and Study Strategies Inventory)* developed by Weinstein, Schulte, and Palmer (1987), are based on current instructional and cognitive research, as well as on information-processing approaches to learning. The LASSI is one of the best-developed and useful instruments currently available to assess students' learning strategies and can be used as a diagnostic and prescriptive tool to help students improve their learning skills. In addition, it has the potential to guide

Table 1. A Taxonomy of Learning Strategies

Cognitive Strategies	*Basic Tasks (e.g., memory for lists)*	*Complex Tasks (e.g., test learning)*
Rehearsal strategies	Reciting list	Shadowing Copy material Verbatim note taking Underlining text
Elaboration strategies	Keywork method Imagery Method of loci Generative note taking Question answering	Paraphrasing Summarizing Creating analogies
Organizational strategies	Clustering Mnemonics	Selecting main idea Outlining Networking Diagramming

Metacognitive Strategies	*All Tasks*
Planning strategies	Setting goals Skimming Generating questions
Monitoring strategies	Self-testing Attention-focus Test-taking strategies
Regulating strategies	Adjusting reading rate Rereading Reviewing Test-taking strategies

Resource Management Strategies	*All Tasks*
Time management	Scheduling Goal setting
Study environment management	Defined area Quiet area Organized area
Effort management	Attributions to effort Mood Self-talk Persistence Self-reinforcement
Support of others	Seeking help from teacher Seeking help from peers Peer/group learning Tutoring

development, implementation, and evaluation of instructional interventions for improving students' learning strategies.

In our work at NCRIPTAL, we have been developing a similar self-report questionnaire (the *Motivated Strategies for Learning Questionnaire,* or MSLQ), based on the integration of motivational and information-processing theories of learning. The higher-order cognitions measured by these learning-strategies instruments (metacognition, active learning, self-regulated learning) should be intended (or, at least, unintended) outcomes of a college education. Therefore, it is important to incorporate constructs based on these information-processing views of student learning into postsecondary assessment programs.

How can instruments developed to measure the student's learning strategies help improve teaching and learning? Although it is assumed that a student's learning strategies will improve during the college career, it is not clear that most college courses will have a direct influence on the student's learning strategies (excluding "learning to learn" courses). Accordingly, in contrast to the cognitive-structure measurement data, the usual aggregate data generated from general learning-strategy questionnaires may not be readily usable by individual faculty members but could be very useful to institutional researchers. The aggregate data could be used at the institutional level to ascertain general skill levels of students and thus to guide curriculum offerings. For example, if a community college finds that many students seldom use effective learning strategies, specific courses might focus on improving learning strategies so that students can benefit more from college. At the level of the individual student, we have found that providing individual feedback about use of learning strategies motivates thinking about skills in a new way. Students discover that these strategies are learnable skills and that academic performance is not totally determined by general ability or intelligence.

The data also could be useful to individual faculty members. For example, an instructor could track how different types of students (classified on the basis of the learning-strategy data) perform in a class over the semester. At the end of the semester, the instructor could compare the learning-strategy patterns of students who did well in the course with patterns of those who did not. This would provide more information to the instructor about the nature of student performance in the class.

Furthermore, patterns in the data might reveal attribute-treatment interactions between types of students, on the one hand, and different methods of instruction, on the other (Corno and Snow, 1986). For example, in a biology class, one type of student may do very well on examinations covering lecture material, while another type of student does very well on the laboratory exercises.

Although there are many practical and logistical aspects of improving an individual course, data on students' learning strategies could help faculty members diagnose the sources of learning problems in their classrooms. Faculty members could assess whether problems in student learning were due to student characteristics (such as motivation or learning skills) or to characteristics of the class (including instructional methods and tasks).

Students' Critical Thinking and Problem Solving. Critical thinking and problem solving are currently hot topics in education, from the elementary through the postsecondary level. A number of books have appeared on the topic (Baron and Sternberg, 1987; Chipman, Segal, and Glaser, 1985; Nickerson, Perkins, and Smith, 1985; Segal, Chipman, and Glaser, 1985) as well as articles (for example, the entire Winter 1984 issue of *Review of Educational Research* deals with problems in the teaching and learning of reasoning skills). Although this attention to the topic is interesting and exciting, there is considerable theoretical confusion concerning the nature of critical thinking and problem solving. Therefore, I will mention several general issues that are relevant to the assessment of critical thinking in postsecondary education.

In an excellent overview of the critical issues involved in attempting to teach general cognitive skills, Glaser (1984) calls attention to five questions that must be considered in future research: Can general cognitive skills be taught? How can current knowledge-based models of cognition be applied to the teaching of general problem-solving skills? How can instruction best be designed to foster general cognitive skills? How can cognitive skills learned in one domain be transferred to another domain? How can we assess the effectiveness of our attempts to teach critical thinking or other general cognitive skills?

The answers to these questions may depend on the orientation of the individuals involved (faculty, institutional researchers, administrators, and so on), but consideration of these issues is important for building programs to assess critical thinking. Thinking about these issues requires individuals to consider their definitions of critical thinking and problem solving, as well as their implicit theories about how students learn these skills and how teachers might teach them. Ideally, these deliberations will produce a local model or theory of how instruction will lead to critical thinking and problem solving. Regardless of its level (course, departmental, institutional), a local model of critical thinking would help to delineate how independent variables (course tasks and activities, curriculum offerings, or institutional dimensions) theoretically influence the dependent variable (students' critical thinking). Assessment programs could then be designed to test this local model. The data from such an assessment program would provide useful feedback to instructors (or to other program designers) about program effectiveness. These data could be used to improve or redesign the critical-thinking instructional program.

This suggestion for the development of local models of instruction and thinking parallels recent work by methodologists working in the area of program evaluation. For example, Cordray (1986) suggests that traditional conceptualizations of treatments and quasi-experimental designs are no longer useful in program evaluation research. Institutional researchers and evaluators should build local conceptual models that specify independent variables (student entry characteristics), exogenous variables, treatment variables (including theoretical as well as practical aspects, such as treatment fidelity and implementation), mediating variables, and outcome variables. The specification of these more theoretical models for postsecondary assessment programs will help to avoid simplistic input-output models of college impact that may be misleading at worst and at best do not provide readily useful information for improving teaching and learning.

A focus on treatment implementation and mediating variables in postsecondary programs to assess critical thinking would highlight the importance of considering variables related to instruction and cognitive processes (the nature of instructional tasks, teacher behavior, students' knowledge structures) as mediators of the impact of college on critical thinking. This focus would help to avoid problems that cannot realistically be expected to result in student progress on a global measure of critical thinking (for example, finding that a specific college curriculum has no influence on students' scores on the Watson-Glaser Critical Thinking Test). At the postsecondary level, it may not matter how the critical-thinking curriculum is labeled or what the course is titled. What will matter is what happens to students in those classes and what they are asked to do that will influence their learning (Doyle, 1983; Pintrich, Cross, Kozma, and McKeachie, 1986). In a course on critical thinking where students only take simple multiple-choice tests and are rarely asked to think critically, it is unlikely that students will learn the skills of critical thinking.

Students' Motivation. One process, or mediating, variable that is almost always ignored or poorly conceptualized in cognitive models of students' learning, critical thinking, or problem solving is motivation. It is clear, however, that initial acquisition of knowledge, as well as transfer of general cognitive skills across different content domains, requires a motivated learner (McKeachie, Pintrich, Lin, and Smith, 1986).

Past models of motivation have not been readily applicable to cognitive models of learning. For example, motivational models based on psychodynamic, drive, or humanistic theories have not been useful for conceptualizing student learning. In addition, motivational models based on basic attitude constructs (values, liking, or interest) have proved too simplistic. In recent years, however, cognitive reformulations of achievement motivation theory have revitalized motivational research and suggested productive relationships between research programs in motivation and cognition (Pintrich, Cross, Kozma, and McKeachie, 1986). Figure 1 displays one version of a general expectancy-value model of motivation that can be used to conceptualize the interactions among motivational, cognitive, and instructional variables (see McKeachie, Pintrich, Lin, and Smith, 1986).

There are two general paths in the model, an expectancy path and a value path. The expectancy path is along the bottom of the figure and includes expectancies, perceived competence, test anxiety, perceptions of task difficulty, and students' beliefs about efficacy, control, and outcome. This aspect of the model subsumes general motivational constructs like self-concept and self-efficacy (students' beliefs about their ability to perform academic tasks). The basic outcome of this path in the model is the student's belief in or expectation of success. The model assumes that students with generally high expectations of success for a specific task (an exam, an assigned paper, or a course) will be more involved in the task and persist longer on the task in the face of difficulty than will students with low expectations of success, who will give up more easily.

At the same time, expectation of success is not the only important motivational component to notice in determining student involvement with the task. The task-value path, along the top of the figure, includes the components *task value* and *student goal*. *Task value* includes three aspects: attainment value, interest value, and utility value. *Attainment value* refers to student's perception of the likelihood that a task will

Figure 1. Components of Motivation

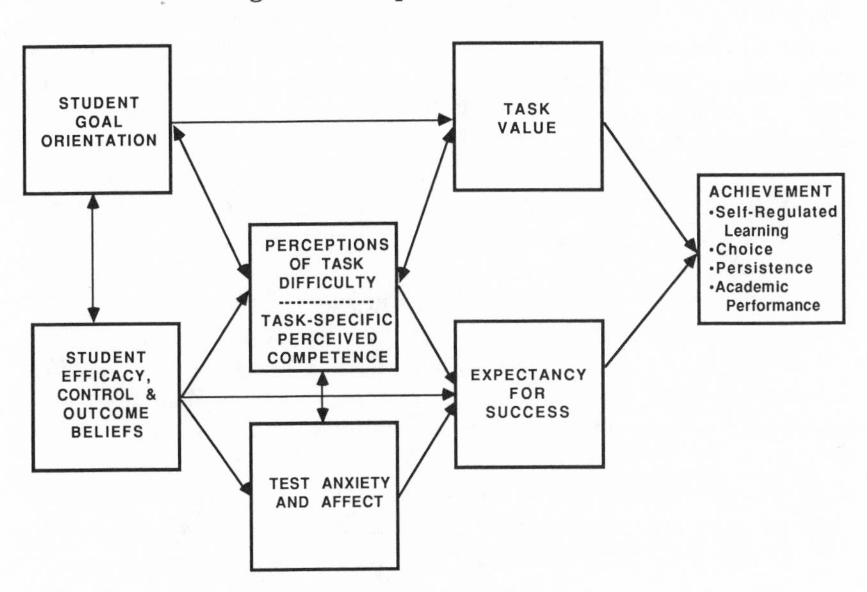

provide a challenge. For example, a student who believes she is smart and perceives doing well in a chemistry course as a challenge would have a high attainment value for the course. *Interest value* includes the student's intrinsic interest in the content of the task (for example, the student enjoys chemistry). Many college courses have the implicit goal of increasing students' intrinsic interest in a discipline. In contrast to the means, or process, aspect of interest value, *utility value* concerns the ends, or instrumental aspect, of a task (that is, the student's perception of the utility of the task for facilitating a specific goal). For example, a student may have no inherent interest in chemistry, but because she has the goal of becoming a doctor and because chemistry is a required course for premedical students, the course has a high utility value for her. This recognition—that tasks may have utility value as well as intrinsic value for students—lessens the need to assume that all instruction has to increase students' intrinsic interest in learning or education.

The other aspect of the task-value path is the student's goals. These goals can include long-term goals (for a career or for life) and short-term goals (for a specific course, paper, or exam). These goals help determine the student's perception of the value of a task, as well as the overall choice of tasks (for example, selecting certain courses). In this model, the value and expectancy components interact to produce student involvement. Both components are assumed to be important predictors of student involvement in college. Assessment models that merely include expectancy components (like self-concept, self-efficacy, or expectation of success) or models that merely include value components (like interest or utility value) will not be so powerful as models that include both expectancy and value components. It is important that assessment programs incorporate these motivational and value components. If assessment systems focus only on narrowly defined cognitive aspects of student performance, they risk missing some of the more intangible aspects of the college experience in terms of students' intrinsic interests and values for learning (Bennett, 1986).

The assessment of motivational constructs has been a continuing research problem. Older models used projective techniques and behavioral observation, but newer cognitive models have relied on self-report instruments (McKeachie, Pintrich, Lin, and Smith, 1986). Although there are problems with self-report instruments (Nisbett and Wilson, 1977), they can be used reliably to tap students' expectations and values. As discussed previously with respect to learning strategies, data from this type of assessment could be used by institutional researchers to determine the relative effects of college experience on students' motivational patterns. In addition, faculty members could tie questionnaire items to specific course content and determine the development or progress in students' interest value for the course material or in students' perceived competence in the course. In addition, using the motivational data, faculty members' explanations' of interactions between students' motivational patterns and their performance could be very helpful for redesigning or improving a course.

Conclusion

Assessment programs can provide one avenue for improving teaching and learning in college settings, if they are closely tied to instructional concerns as well as to current theory on cognitive models of student learning (Haney, 1984; Linn, 1986; Sternberg, 1985). Accordingly, if institutional researchers and administrators are serious about improving postsecondary teaching and learning, and if they plan to use assessment programs as one tool to reach this goal, then the assessment programs must be linked to strong theoretical frameworks of student learning, motivation, and instruction. If an assessment programs is basically atheoretical in nature, includes a variety of items tapping a diversity of student outcomes, and is not linked to concerns of teaching and learning, then it will not be very useful for improving teaching and learning in higher education.

Although other models may also be useful for designing assessment programs, the general information-processing model presented in this chapter seems to be one of the most relevant theoretical models. It is important to note that useful models should be concerned not only with the psychology of student learning and development but also with the psychology of instruction. In addition, simple input-output models of college teaching and learning are not adequate for most instructional improvement efforts. Assessment programs need to focus not only on student outcomes but also on instructional processes and activities, as well as on such other student mediating variables as knowledge structures, learning strategies, and motivation. If assessment programs focus on the links between actual instructional processes and mediating variables and outcomes, then the information generated will be more useful for actual improvement efforts. This process-oriented approach will help the field move beyond the identification of instructional problems to practical suggestions for instructional design and improvement.

References

Baron, J., and Sternberg, R. *Teaching Thinking Skills.* New York: Freeman, 1987.

Bennett, W. J. "Foreword." In C. Adelman (ed.), *Assessment in American Higher Education: Issues and Contexts.* Washington, D.C.: U.S. Government Printing Office, 1986.

Bok, D. *Higher Learning.* Cambridge, Mass.: Harvard University Press, 1986.

Boyer, E. *College: The Undergraduate Experience in America.* New York: Harper & Row, 1987.

Bransford, J., Sherwood, R., Vye, N., and Rieser, J. "Teaching Thinking and Problem-Solving: Research Foundations." *American Psychologist,* 1986, *41,* 1078–1089.

Brown, W. *Effective Study Test.* San Marcos, Tex.: Effective Study Materials, 1964.

Brown, W., and Holtzman, W. *Survey of Study Habits and Attitudes.* New York: The Psychological Corporation, 1967.

Carter, J. *California Study Methods Survey.* Monterey, Calif.: California Test Bureau, 1958.

Chi, M. "Knowledge Structures and Memory Development." In R. Siegler (ed.), *Children's Thinking: What Develops?* Hillsdale, N.J.: Erlbaum, 1978.

Chipman, S., Segal, J., and Glaser, R. *Thinking and Learning Skills: Research Issues.* Vol. 2. Hillsdale, N.J.: Erlbaum, 1985.

Christensen, F. *College Adjustment and Study Skills Inventory.* Berea, Ohio: Personal Growth Press, 1968.

Cook, T., and Campbell, D. *Quasi-Experimentation: Design and Analysis Issues for Field Settings.* Chicago: Rand McNally, 1979.

Cordray, D. "Quasi-Experimental Analysis: A Mixture of Methods and Judgment." In W. Trochim (ed.), *Advances in Quasi-Experimental Design and Analysis.* New Directions for Program Evaluation, no. 31. San Francisco: Jossey-Bass, 1986.

Corno, L., and Mandinach, E. "The Role of Cognitive Engagement in Classroom Learning and Motivation." *Educational Psychologist,* 1983, *18,* 88–100.

Corno, L., and Snow, R. "Adapting Teaching to Individual Differences Among Learners." In M. Wittrock (ed.), *Handbook of Research on Teaching.* New York: Macmillan, 1986.

Dansereau, D. "Learning Strategy Research." In J. Segal, S. Chipman, and R. Glaser (eds.), *Thinking and Learning Skills: Relating Instruction to Research.* Vol. 1. Hillsdale, N.J.: Erlbaum, 1985.

Doyle, W. "Academic Work." *Review of Educational Research,* 1983, *53,* 159–199.

Glaser, R. "Education and Thinking: The Role of Knowledge." *American Psychologist,* 1984, *39,* 93–104.

Goldman, R., and Warren, R. "Discriminant Analysis of Study Strategies Connected with College Grade Success in Different Major Fields." *Journal of Educational Measurement,* 1973, *10,* 39–47.

Haney, W. "Testing Reasoning and Reasoning About Testing." *Review of Educational Research,* 1984, *54,* 597–654.

Linn, R. "Educational Testing and Assessment: Research Needs and Policy Issues." *American Psychologist,* 1986, *41,* 1153–1160.

McKeachie, W. J., Pintrich, P. R., Lin, Y., and Smith, D. *Teaching and Learning in the College Classroom: A Review of the Research Literature.* Ann Arbor: National Center for Research to Improve Postsecondary Teaching and Learning, University of Michigan, 1986.

Naveh-Benjamin, M., McKeachie, W. J., Lin, Y., and Tucker, D. "Inferring Students' Cognitive Structure and Their Development Using the 'Ordered-Tree Technique.'" *Journal of Educational Psychology,* 1986, *78,* 130–140.

Nickerson, R., Perkins, D., and Smith, E. *The Teaching of Thinking.* Hillsdale, N.J.: Erlbaum, 1985.

NIE Study Group on the Conditions of Excellence in American Higher Education. *Involvement in Learning: Realizing the Potential of American Higher Education.* Washington, D.C.: U.S. Government Printing Office, 1984.

Nisbett, R., and Wilson, T. "Telling More Than We Can Know: Verbal Reports on Mental Processes." *Psychological Review,* 1977, *84,* 231–259.

Paris, S., Lipson, M., and Wixson, K. "Becoming a Strategic Reader." *Contemporary Educational Psychology,* 1983, *8,* 293–316.

Pintrich, P. R., Cross, D., Kozma, R., and McKeachie, W. J. "Instructional Psychology." *Annual Review of Psychology,* 1986, *37,* 611–651.

Pressley, M. "The Relevance of the Good Strategy User Model to the Teaching of Mathematics." *Educational Psychologist,* 1986, *21,* 139–161.

Segal, J., Chipman, S., and Glaser, R. *Thinking and Learning Skills: Relating Instruction to Research.* Vol. 1. Hillsdale, N.J.: Erlbaum, 1985.

Shavelson, R. "On Quagmires, Philosophical and Otherwise: A Reply to Phillips." *Educational Psychologist,* 1983, *18,* 81–87.

Siegler, R. *Children's Thinking.* Englewood Cliffs, N.J.: Prentice-Hall, 1986.

Sternberg, R. *Beyond IQ: A Triarchic Theory of Human Intelligence.* Cambridge, Mass.: Cambridge University Press, 1985.

Tobias, S. "When Do Instructional Methods Make a Difference?" *Educational Researcher,* 1982, *11,* 4–10.

Weinstein, C., and Mayer, R. "The Teaching of Learning Strategies." In M. Wittrock (ed.), *Handbook of Research on Teaching.* New York: Macmillan, 1986.

Weinstein, C., Schulte, A., and Palmer, D. *LASSI: The Learning and Study Strategies Inventory.* Clearwater, Florida: H & H Publishing, 1987.

Weinstein, C., and Underwood, V. "Learning Strategies: The How of Learning." In J. Segal, S. Chipman, and R. Glaser (eds.), *Thinking and Learning Skills: Relating Instruction to Research.* Vol. 1. Hillsdale, N.J.: Erlbaum, 1985.

Paul R. Pintrich is assistant professor in the Curriculum, Teaching, and Psychological Studies Department in the School of Education and associate director of the Teaching and Learning Research Program in the National Center for Research to Improve Postsecondary Teaching and Learning (NCRIPTAL), at the University of Michigan.

By increasing research activities focused directly on teaching and learning issues, institutional researchers are expanding their professional role.

Critical Directions for the Future

Lisa A. Mets, Joan S. Stark

The 1980s are placing institutional researchers before a new threshold. In the past twenty-five years, the institutional research field has developed from infancy through adolescence and is now approaching maturity. Like young adults, institutional researchers are faced with difficult decisions about directions to pursue, particularly concerning which aspects of institutional study to include in their work.

To avoid fragmentation of the field in the face of many possible options, Marvin W. Peterson has suggested the need for a common view of practice and a common professional theme. Regarding the common view of practice, he offered the following view: "It is appropriate to conceive of the field as encompassing an institutional *process* involving *information* collection or development (including technology), *analysis or research,* and *utilization* activities designed to *improve* some aspect of an institution of higher education" (AIR Presidential Panel, 1985, p. 25; see also Peterson, 1985; Muffo and McLaughlin, 1987). He suggested the following dimensions for the common professional theme: (1) a concern for *improvement* in institutional functioning, (2) a concern for relating *theory to practice,* and (3) a concern for *responsiveness* (demonstrated by attacking new problems, playing new roles, and adopting appropriate new methods) (AIR Presidential Panel, 1985, p. 26).

J. S. Stark and L. A. Mets (eds.). *Improving Teaching and Learning Through Research.*
New Directions for Institutional Research, no. 57. San Francisco: Jossey-Bass, Spring 1988.

The fact that this issue of *New Directions for Institutional Research* brings both theoretical and practical perspectives to the study and enhancement of teaching and learning illustrates that the profession has a common view of practice and a unifying theme, as defined by Peterson. In suggesting types of information to be collected and analyses to be performed, the authors of this volume have asserted that institutional researchers can maintain a strong sense of purpose and a distinct identity while being responsive to new types of institutional improvement issues. In the final analysis, whether research results will be utilized to bring about improvement may depend on the strength of collaborative efforts and must be demonstrated in the unique context of each campus.

In each of the preceding chapters, the authors have shared approaches to teaching and learning improvement being pursued through their research projects in the National Center for Research to Improve Postsecondary Teaching and Learning (NCRIPTAL). More important, however, both individually and collectively they have suggested ways in which institutional researchers can contribute to research and practice that improves teaching and learning. All of the authors agree that institutional researchers need to keep abreast of emerging theories, examining them in the contexts of their own institutions; that they increasingly must integrate varied research methodologies; and, finally, that they must extend their collaboration in research to include those conducting basic research and those developing academic policy, not only in their own institutions but also among institutions and in public forums.

In this final chapter, we attempt to assist our readers in their work by reviewing several important issues that compel attention to improvement of teaching and learning, summarizing some positive changes that seem likely to occur in the field of institutional research if the challenges described in this volume are accepted, describing some instruments emerging from work at NCRIPTAL that may become useful tools for institutional researchers, and suggesting sources of additional reading for those who desire to expand their background in any of the areas of research discussed in this volume.

Compelling Critical Issues

During the past two decades, institutional research activities focused on the management functions of the institution. It is becoming increasingly apparent that for the remainder of this decade and the next, institutional research activities may focus on teaching and learning functions. This seems likely because several important issues compel attention to this type of research. Some of these issues are the following.

Accountability. *Accountability* has never been a stronger watchword in higher education than it is today. Recently, accountability initiatives have focused less on how public money is spent and more on whether the public is getting its money's worth. The quality of education has been seriously questioned by public representatives. From federal to local levels, this question is being asked: "Is a college education meeting its expected standards?"

Assessing Effectiveness. In varied forms, assessment has long been a predominant mechanism for achieving accountability. Higher education systems, institutions, and programs all have been assessed for their fiscal efficiency and for how well they are meeting established societal goals and standards. Thus, *institutional effectiveness* has referred to how well institutions have managed themselves, responded to demands, and utilized resources. Placed in this context, the current emphasis on direct assessment of teaching and learning is a natural extension of previously accepted practice. Now the term *effectiveness* is being applied to teaching and learning.

Increasing Demands for Data. With better technology facilitating the gathering, documentation, and analysis of data, requests for more and better information are increasing, from constituencies within the institution as well as from external agencies. For example, with implementation of assessment programs come attendant requests for release of assessment results. Calls for proof of improved teaching and learning may now include not only the reporting of test scores on various entrance and exit examinations but also reports of other quantifiable indicators.

Expanding Technology and Research. With the increasing use of microcomputers, the adoption of user-friendly software allowing sophisticated analyses, and increasing access to data, the number of researchers is increasing and the questions posed are more varied. More and better research on the teaching and learning functions in college can be conducted. Institutional researchers no longer have inside access to data.

Minority Participation in Higher Education. The decreasing participation rate of more and more minority populations already demands the attention of the higher education community. Research that helps to increase the responsiveness of colleges and universities to the educational needs of minorities is a teaching and learning issue, not a management issue.

Implications for Institutional Research

The approaches that individual institutional researchers will take in response to the compelling issues already mentioned will be determined by how directly involved researchers become in improving teaching and learning functions. For those who now primarily provide data for management decisions about effectiveness and efficiency, it is a long leap to exploring teaching and learning issues. However, for institutional researchers currently conducting studies of retention/attrition, student flow, or student achievement, activities to examine the quality of teaching and learning are a short next step. Whether the leap is long or short, direct or indirect, we predict that most institutional researchers will be involved to some extent with teaching and learning issues during the next decade. Thus, we now suggest a few implications of their involvement for institutional research as a field.

Broadened Research Base. As more collaborative activities are developed between institutional researchers and the corps of basic researchers already conducting studies on teaching and learning, the databases available to institutional research, as well as the field's horizons, will broaden. Because many basic researchers are faculty members, opportunities exist to make the work of institutional researchers more visible, as the two types of researchers share the same laboratory space: the institution.

Comparative Research. Recalling Green and Stark's categorization of research-intervention points to improve teaching and learning (see Chapter One), we note that while actors and organizational contexts may vary, teaching and learning processes are likely to be similar, even in diverse institutions. Thus, as increasing numbers of institutional and basic researchers use common variables and share their work, comparative research should lead to a consistent and growing body of knowledge about improvement of teaching and learning.

Integration of Research Methodologies. As institutional researchers study the improvement of teaching and learning, the nature of the questions asked will require the integration of several research methodologies. Basic research, policy analysis, and evaluation research will all contribute to the methodology adopted by the institutional researcher. Thus, the relationship among these types of research generally should become more symbiotic.

Translation of Theory into Practice. Because of their proximity to faculty and to students involved in the teaching and learning processes, institutional researchers will have new opportunities to facilitate transitions from research findings to innovative practices.

Useful Instruments Emerging from NCRIPTAL

Each of the research teams at NCRIPTAL is conducting studies to improve understanding of ways in which teaching and learning can be improved. Thus, according to the methods chosen, each team has developed and pilot-tested research instruments based on theoretical dimensions that have been judged important. Several of these research instruments, when accompanied by appropriate explanatory guidebooks, can be made useful both for data collection and for fruitful discussion on campuses. In keeping with its mission to encourage both active research and educational improvement, NCRIPTAL plans to make these instruments available at cost to the higher education community. When the instruments are ready, institutional researchers may wish to use them in their investigations or recommend them to faculty and instructional development offices. Although neither the titles of final versions nor the dates of availability are firm at this time, we anticipate being more definite by the fall of 1988. The following sections describe what institutional researchers can expect from the researchers who are authors of this volume.

Academic Management Practices Self-Study. Based on completed pilot surveys, Marvin W. Peterson and Kim S. Cameron are constructing a checklist of academic management practices that college administrators believe support (or fail to support) teaching and learning. Another instrument, currently being prepared for extensive pilot testing, will measure three dimensions of academic climate: supportiveness for academic innovation and change, supportiveness of the academic workplace, and supportiveness of academic management practices.

The Course Planning Exploration is a questionnaire, developed under the direction of Joan S. Stark and Malcolm A. Lowther, to ascertain important influences on faculty course planning. Currently, it is being used to survey faculty who teach introductory courses in twelve fields in a nationally representative sample of colleges and universities. A campus discussion guide will describe possible uses of the ideas the survey incorporates. As a survey or interview, it helps to identify resources and information faculty believe they lack or do not find helpful for course planning. As a stimulus to discussion, it may be useful in faculty development groups or at departmental meetings concerning basic educational beliefs of faculty members that influence how they select and arrange course content. A database now being developed will allow faculty members to compare their own views with the views of others in their disciplines and college types. A theoretically parallel course syllabus guide also is being field-tested.

Faculty Perceptions of the Teaching Role, an instrument developed under the supervision of Robert T. Blackburn and Janet H. Lawrence, is currently being used in a national survey of college faculty. The instrument is designed to measure four important sets of faculty perceptions: self-competence assessment, incentive value of evaluation and reward policies and practices, adequacy of institutional resources, and attributes of effective administrators. When used by institutional researchers with respect to instruction, the items can provide insights into faculty views about the teaching-learning process, particularly about how much they believe teaching is valued at their respective colleges and the extent to which different forms of evaluation may influence changes in teaching. A comparative information base is now being built.

The Motivated Student Learning Questionnaire, developed under the leadership of Wilbert J. McKeachie and Paul R. Pintrich, will be useful in measuring student motivation as well as student use of varied learning strategies. It helps classroom instructors to assist students in improving their learning strategies and their motivation to learn, as well as to measure changes in these two attributes. During 1987–1988, the instrument is being tested in several college classrooms at three diverse institutions.

Selected Sources for Further Reading

Although the authors of this volume have cited specific works in their discussions, some readers may wish to pursue additional sources related to one or more of the topics in this volume. To assist all types of researchers, each research team at NCRIPTAL developed literature syntheses relevant to the college subenvironments they are studying (see Figure 1, Editors' Notes). These reviews, listed below for easy reference, contain comprehensive bibliographies of materials related directly or indirectly to improving teaching and learning. All were published in 1986 and are available at cost of production and postage from NCRIPTAL, 2400 School of Education Building, University of Michigan, Ann Arbor, Michigan 48109-1259.

Wilbert J. McKeachie, Paul R. Pintrich, Yi-Guang Lin, and David A. F. Smith. *Teaching and Learning in the College Classroom: A Review of the Research Literature* (NCRIPTAL Report 86-B-001.0).

Joan S. Stark and Malcolm A. Lowther. *Designing the Learning Plan: A Review of Research and Theory Related to College Curricula* (NCRIPTAL Report 86-C-001.0).

Robert T. Blackburn, Janet H. Lawrence, Steven Ross, Virginia Polk Okoloko, Jeffrey P. Bieber, Rosalie Meiland, and Terry Street. *Faculty as a Key Resource: A Review of the Research Literature* (NCRIPTAL Report 86-D-001.0).

Marvin W. Peterson, Kim S. Cameron, Lisa A. Mets, Philip Jones, and Deborah Ettington. *The Organizational Context for Teaching and Learning: A Review of the Research Literature* (NCRIPTAL Report 86-E-001.0).

While not research reviews, three additional NCRIPTAL papers may be useful to institutional researchers.

Harold A. Korn. *Psychological Models of the Impact of College on Students* (NCRIPTAL Report 86-B-002.0).

This report discusses five perspectives on the impact of college on students, along with theoretical and methodological issues these perspectives raise. Two theoretical models, based in cognitive psychology, and issues that must be addressed before the impact of college on the lives of individual students can be studied are presented by the author.

Joanne M. Alexander and Joan S. Stark. *Focusing on Student Academic Outcomes: A Working Paper* (NCRIPTAL Report 86-A-002.0).

The current movement to assess college student educational outcomes changes its character almost daily. Thus, while no publication can be entirely current, this working paper cuts through some of the definitional confusion by considering assessment as a process of measurement and evaluation with eight identifiable parameters. The paper incorporates the rationale behind NCRIPTAL's decision to focus its studies primarily on cognitive development of college students.

Carol D. Vogel and Joan S. Stark. *Postsecondary Teaching and Learning Issues in Search of Researchers: A Working Paper* (NCRIPTAL Report 86-A-003.0).

This working paper goes beyond the issues of teaching/learning improvement that NCRIPTAL researchers are currently studying, to suggest a wide variety of related issues that other researchers might address.

Conclusion

During the past quarter-century, institutional researchers have supported the teaching and learning functions of institutions somewhat indirectly; that is, since much of their research was directed at helping to strengthen institutional management functions, institutional researchers could legitimately argue that an effectively run institution probably produces teaching and learning outcomes effectively. However, it has been suggested recently that even institutions that are well managed may not be achieving their potential with today's students. Furthermore, as pointed out in Chapter Two, little research has been discovered to support the relationship postulated between effective management and effective education. In this context, new studies that involve institutional research more directly seem particularly appropriate.

Institutional researchers today must consider the extent to which they should become more directly involved in studying and improving the teaching and learning functions. In this volume, we have argued that they should take an active role. We submit that by being responsive to current concerns about teaching and learning improvement, institutional researchers are expanding their role, not changing it, and are capitalizing on important opportunities, rather than forgoing them. In light of the primary mission of colleges and universities, such a role expansion seems timely and consistent with past growth and development of institutional research. By joining the ranks of those who study educational processes directly, institutional research does not fragment its functions; rather, institutional research can move "to a new level of development" (AIR Presidential Panel, 1985, p. 22).

References

AIR Presidential Panel. "Institutional Research in Transition: Proliferation or Professional Integration." In *Promoting Excellence Through Information and Technology.* General session presentations of the 25th Anniversary Forum of the Association for Institutional Research. Tallahassee, Fla.: Association for Institutional Research, 1985.

Muffo, J. A., and McLaughlin, G. W. *A Primer on Institutional Research.* Tallahassee, Fla.: Association for Institutional Research, 1987.

Peterson, M. W. "Institutional Research: An Evolutionary Perspective." In M. W. Peterson and M. Corcoran (eds.), *Institutional Research in Transition.* New Directions for Institutional Research, no. 46. San Francisco: Jossey-Bass, 1985.

Lisa A. Mets is assistant to the vice-president for administration and planning at Northwestern University. She is currently a doctoral candidate in higher education at the University of Michigan and was formerly a research associate in the Center for the Study of Higher and Postsecondary Education and the National Center for Research to Improve Postsecondary Teaching and Learning (NCRIPTAL), at the University of Michigan.

Joan S. Stark is professor of higher education, a researcher in the Center for the Study of Higher and Postsecondary Education, and director of the National Center for Research to Improve Postsecondary Teaching and Learning (NCRIPTAL), at the University of Michigan.

Index